Walk on the Wild Side

Off the beaten track in Southern Scotland with Mary Hayward

Often these walks are off the beaten track – across streams, over fences, on rough terrain. These adventures are not of an extreme kind but they do require a certain degree of agility and stamina. Even with these, accidents can happen. Please, be aware that you follow these pleasant, sometimes exciting, routes at your own risk. The author takes no responsibility for any unpleasant outcomes. The rewarding results she is happy to admit may be down to her!

Route maps prepared by Mary Hayward
Photographs by various and © of the owners

Design by GSB (Edinburgh)

Contains OS data © Crown copyright
and database right 2017

Cover photograph: Above St Mary's Loch

For my Family

"What would the world be, once bereft

Of wet and of wildness? Let them be left,

O let them be left, wildness and wet;

Long live the weeds and the wilderness yet."

Gerard Manley Hopkins, 1881

Acknowledgements

Who has helped me? It's a long list and I hope, on using this book, the members do not feel their efforts have been wasted.

Who kicked a**** to get me started? That was Liz Ballantyne. Without complaint she has helped to check the routes in hail, rain and shine. She roped her husband, Scott, in with his magical graphic abilities. I am amazed how good he can make a scruffy outline look. Thank you both.

Then there are the members of the Edinburgh U3A Adventure Walking Group. They have checked, walked and commented encouragingly on my ideas. Many of them have shared their pictures with me, especially Liam McDowell. Most of the pictures in the book are his. Thank you all.

Ordnance Survey were very helpful and understanding on the phone guiding me through their website. Their 1:25,000 paper maps along with their free 'OS Locate' app are the perfect walking companions in the field.

Who has been there all the time, encouraging, helping and de-stressing? My family, of course. A special mention must be made of my 6 year old grandson, Larry, who has taken many of these pictures with his little camera. He has an eye for composition which did not come from Granny. Daddy Larry proof-read and advised with patience and endless encouragement.

Thank you all.

Mary Hayward   May 2017

The good walker's code

Multi Task!

- Check the ground in front of your feet.
- Look ahead for obstacles, Oops!, of any kind.
- Look for flowers.
- Look for birds.
- Listen to everything.

Oops!

Stop!   Be Quiet!   Assess!   Respect!

Avoid completely: bulls, cows with young calves, sheep giving birth or with young lambs, horses. Be safe.

Wide Berth: all other animals. Do not disturb.

Land owner: smile, listen, if possible co-operate BUT remember the law allows you to be there.

Crops: never walk on crops. Find a way round.

Fences: climb at a strong post or squeeze through.

Gates: if you have to, climb at the hinge end. Leave them as you find them.

Streams: find the narrowest place – upstream?

Difficult terrain: note a target point ahead and work out the easiest route.

Behave with Respect
Do no damage

5

Planning your walk

Be Safe

Check weather forecast

www.metoffice.gov.uk
www.mwis.org.uk
www.mountain-forecast.com

Look at wind speed and direction; cloud level; precipitation; freezing level. Remember what was a pleasant summer ramble can become a life-threatening experience in the high winds, low visibility, snow or ice of winter.
Choose your area depending on the weather.

Look at the Locations Map on page 9 What walks are available in your chosen area?

Check available walks' statistics How many daylight hours have you got? Remember to leave at least one hour as a safety margin in case of accident. Think of the slowest member of the group.
How high does each walk go? Weather conditions at that altitude? Choose your walk.

Photocopy your chosen walk Leave the book with someone and a note of which walk you're doing. (Or better still, make sure they own a copy!)
Say when you expect to be back. Say who is with you.

The right equipment Do you and all members of your group have:
- 1:25,000 OS map in a waterproof case, attached to you;
- Compass attached to you;
- Instructions;
- Fully charged phone with 'OS Locate' app on it;
- Strong, appropriate footwear with good treads especially on the heel edge;
- Full rainwear;
- Survival bag;
- Food;
- Emergency food;
- Water;
- Emergency clothing;
- Watch;
- Money;
- Perhaps crampons or spikes;
- Perhaps sticks;
- Reliable transport;
- Emergency contact numbers for each other;
- Possibly fully charged GPS?

Remember – do not rely solely on battery operated devices.

Key to the walks

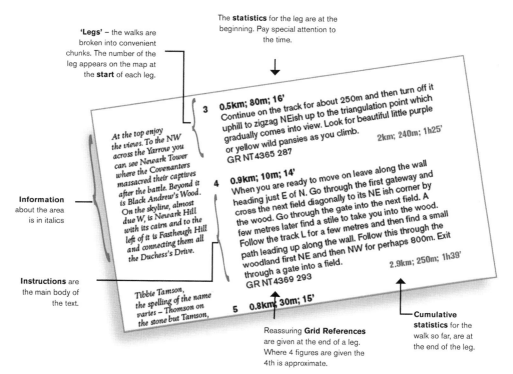

'Legs' – the walks are broken into convenient chunks. The number of the leg appears on the map at the **start** of each leg.

The **statistics** for the leg are at the beginning. Pay special attention to the time.

Information about the area is in italics

Instructions are the main body of the text.

3 **0.5km; 80m; 16'**
Continue on the track for about 250m and then turn off it uphill to zigzag NEish up to the triangulation point which gradually comes into view. Look for beautiful little purple or yellow wild pansies as you climb.   2km; 240m; 1h25'
GR NT 4365 287

At the top enjoy the views. To the NW across the Yarrow you can see Newark Tower where the Covenanters massacred their captives after the battle. Beyond it is Black Andrew's Wood. On the skyline, almost due W, is Newark Hill with its cairn and to the left of it is Fastheugh Hill and connecting them all the Duchess's Drive.

4 **0.9km; 10m; 14'**
When you are ready to move on leave along the wall heading just E of N. Go through the first gateway and cross the next field diagonally to its NE ish corner by the wood. Go through the gate into the next field. A few metres later find a stile to take you into the wood. Follow the track L for a few metres and then find a small path leading up along the wall. Follow this through the woodland first NE and then NW for perhaps 800m. Exit through a gate into a field.   2.9km; 250m; 1h39'
GR NT 4369 293

Tibbie Tamson, the spelling of the name varies – Thomson on the stone but Tamson,

5 **0.8km; 30m; 15'**

Reassuring **Grid References** are given at the end of a leg. Where 4 figures are given the 4th is approximate.

Cumulative statistics for the walk so far, are at the end of the leg.

Notes on other key points

- Directions are from Edinburgh.
- Sketch maps give the general shape of the walk. For accuracy use OS 1:25,000.
- Where a walk returns to a point an * is used to indicate this – e.g bridge* means you will return to this bridge later.
- Magnetic declineation is 1° or 2° – well within compass error – so no corrections have been made.

Abbreviations

- Distances are in kilometres, km, or metres, m.
- Ascents are in metres, m.
- Time is in hours, h, and minutes, '. For example 2 hours and 16 minutes is abbreviated to 2h16'.
- Time taken, estimated at 4km/h and 1' for every 10m ascent, is rounded up for each leg.
- E-ish, for example, means in an overall easterly direction.

> **Please note the maps are not to scale and provide a rough guide only.**
> **1:25,000 OS maps and a compass are vital.**

List of Contents

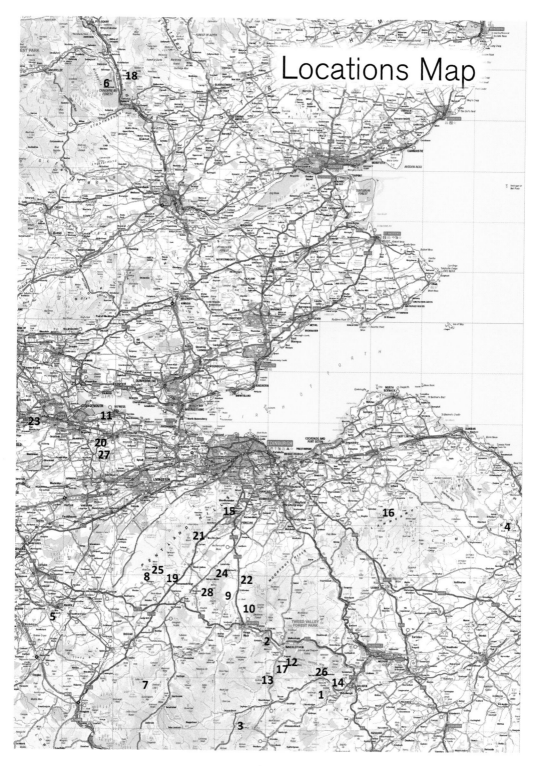

Locations Map

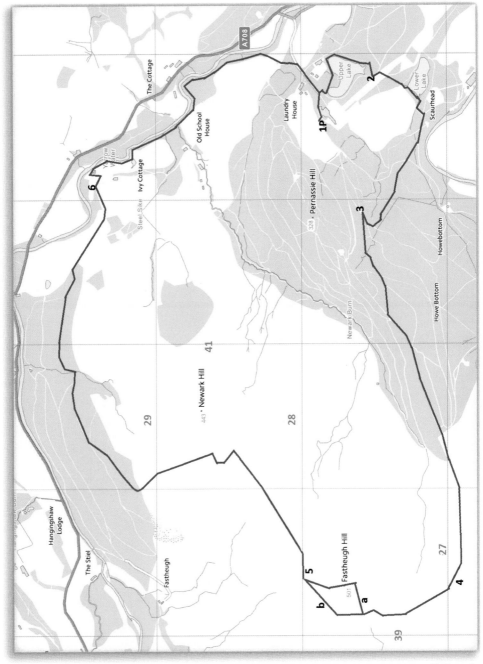

Not to scale

1 • BOWHILL
Duchess' Drive and more.

A moderate walk in the Buccleuch Estate by lochs, through woodland, over open moorland and by the riverside. There is no charge if you go in the off-season when the house is closed. Check on-line for dates – opening times are roughly Easter to October.

Mute swans

WE SAW in March: goshawk displaying, goldeneye, tufted duck, mute swans, bullfinch, buzzards, kestrel, skylarks singing, dippers.

MAP OS Explorer **337** Peebles and Innerleithen and OS Explorer **338** Galashiels, Selkirk and Melrose. The walk spans both maps.

Distance 13.8km
Ascent 420m
Walking Time 4h10'
Allow 5h10'
Highest Elevation 500m

PARK In Bowhill car park. Grid Reference NT426 278. Post code TD7 5ET. No toilets here.

TO GET THERE, avoiding Selkirk, take the A7 south from Edinburgh. Pass through the small hamlet of Stow and about 5mls further turn right on to B710 signposted Clovenfords. When you reach that village take the A72 exit from the roundabout and IMMEDIATELY turn L on to Caddonfoot Road, the B710 continued. At Caddonfoot turn L on to the A707. Follow it south, across the Tweed and on through the outskirts of Selkirk. The road does a sharp L bend. Immediately afterwards turn R on to the A708 indicating St Mary's Loch. Now you will pass The Waterwheel Café (coffee later) and Salmon Leap Viewing Centre on the left, the entrance to Philipshaugh on the right and finally, on the left, the entrance to Bowhill. Go up the avenue to the house and then follow the car park signs.

CAFÉ The Waterwheel Cafe, 0175022258. GR NT450 277. It is on the A708 beside the Salmon Leap Viewing Centre and just about opposite Philipshaugh Garden entrance. Ring one or two days ahead to tell them when and how many. On the OS map it is marked as Old Mill Farm. They make excellent applecake.

THE WALK

1 1km; 0m; 15'

Leave the car park and turn R back down the drive, E-ish. Pass the entrance to the courtyard and then take the first R, down towards the Upper Loch. The walk has some black markers but don't depend on them – some are missing. Almost immediately branch L off the tarmac. Follow the paths round the loch to the south end from where you will have a clear view of the house across the water.

Bowhill is the home of the Duke and Duchess of Buccleuch and Queensberry. The land has been in the hands of the Scott family on and off since 1322 when a Bruce gifted it to them. Legend has it that the name Buccleuch dates back to the 10th century when a John Scott saved King Kenneth III who was trapped in a ravine by a charging buck. Buccleuch means the 'buck of the cleuch'. The present house was built in 1812 and extended later in that century under the guidance of a team of architects including David Bryce who did Portmore House (See Walk 22). Sir Walter Scott was a frequent visitor. He enjoyed the house so much that he suggested forming the Upper Loch to reflect its beauty. The house served as a military hospital during World War Two.

Continue to a tarmac roadway where you pick up signs, still black, to the Lower Loch. Turn L.
GR NT478 275   1km; 0m; 15'

The Duchess' Drive was constructed as a carriageway for Anne, Duchess of Monmouth and Buccleuch. You may spot milestones as you walk. Duchess Anne had the Buccleuch title in her own right and became Duchess of Monmouth when she married the Duke of Monmouth, son of Charles II. She it was who began to conserve the forest protecting it from illegal logging.

2 2.1km; 90m; 40'

Follow the tarmac road down ignoring black markers directing you to the left. When you have an open field on your right turn L down to the Lower Loch. Walk past the west end of the loch to find a picturesque boathouse. Walk ahead leaving the loch behind and ascend to a tarmac road. Go W. You will see, tucked away on your left, a white house and soon find a fork on the road. Take the right branch signed Bowhill. A few metres further on, go across the crossroads to leave the tarmac. Follow the broad track up through the forest as it ascends just N of W for 1.3km. Stick to your direction ignoring all other branches. Finally your track swings N to reach a T junction with the Duchess' Drive. It has a labelled post.
GR NT418 275   3.1km; 90m; 55'

The ruined 16th century Aikwood Tower was restored as a family home by Sir David Steel, a member of the Scott clan. His son now lets it out as holiday 'cottage'.

3 2.7km; 210m; 1h

Turn L, W. Follow the Drive west through the forest. As you walk you may catch a glimpse of Aikwood Tower to the south on the other bank of the Ettrick. 1.7km of forest walk brings you to a gate. You may want to eat lunch in the shelter of the wall before you head out across the wild hillside. Go through the gate and continue westward

Reed Bunting

Newark Tower dates from the 15th century with its defensive barmkin dating from the 16th century. Later it was a royal hunting lodge and the king's crest can still be seen on the west wall. In 1645, after the Battle of Philipshaugh when the Covenanters routed the Duke of Montrose's Royalist troops, the captives, imprisoned in the tower, were slaughtered and buried in Slain Men's Lea which lies a little further on between the old school house and the River Yarrow.

up across the moorland with a wall on your right until 1km later there is a right fork. Take this fork.
GR NT394 269   5.8km; 300m; 1h55'

4   1.1km; 70m; 24'

Go through the gate in the wall and head NW-ish across the land where the Newark Burn rises. As the track ascends round Fastheugh Hill you come to another fork* in the path. Here you have a choice of routes.
GR NT392 275

a) On a beautiful calm day, you may wish to follow the boundary wall up NE to Coplaw Cairn. From the cairn cross the broken-down fence and ascend just W of N on faint paths through the heather to reach the top of Fastheugh Hill. GR NT393 277.

Descend N-ish to regain the Duchess' Drive. Turn R on it.

b) If the weather is wild you may prefer to stay on the Drive going left at the fork* mentioned above and passing through the gate to follow round the hill instead of over it. This alternative removes 35m ascent from your statistics.
GR NT396 280   6.9km; 370m; 2h19'

5   4.5km; 0m; 1h10'

Continue to descend on the broad track of the Duchess' Drive, following blue markers, and taking the L fork at GR NT403 285 as it descends north into Black Andrew Wood. You may see the Moffat Hills to the west as you walk. As you leave the wood you join a tarmac road. Follow it E and after about 250m turn left to visit the remains of Newark Tower. Have a look around it.
GR NT421 294   11.4km; 370m; 3h29'

6   2.4km; 50m; 41'

Continue on the same track ascending S-ish for perhaps 100m, turn sharp left and descend rapidly to swing past some cottages and reach the Yarrow. Walk S-ish along the riverside path. The field on your right is Slain Men's Lea. Follow the beautiful path for about 1.8km. Finally it leaves the river and takes you across the field between two rows of magnificent lime trees. Follow them to the roadway. Cross and take the side road opposite to lead you back to the car park.
13.8km; 420m; 4h10'

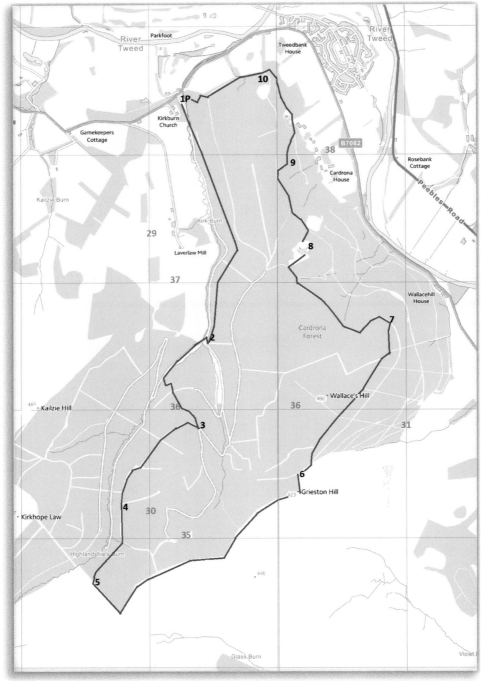

Not to scale

2 • CARDRONA

A walk in forest and moorland including a short version for inclement weather. A prehistoric fort, pele tower housing bats. Wonderful views.

Heron

BEFORE doing this walk you can check for logging activities by calling 01387860247

MAP OS Explorer **337**, Peebles & Innerleithen

Distance 12.5km
Ascent 485m
Walking Time 4h **(shorter version 3h)**
Allow 5h
Highest Elevation 480m

PARK Forestry Commission car park serving Kirkburn Forest. GR NT2925 3845

TO GET THERE Drive to Peebles. Turn R through the town. At the end of the High St. turn L across the bridge. At the other side keep L parallel to the river and beside a large car park. Drive towards Cardrona. Notice, at a right bend in the road, the entrance to Kailzie. You will return here for coffee. A little later the road descends. At the bottom, on the R, suddenly you will find the car park. There is a small charge.

TOILETS may be open by the car park.

CAFÉ Kailzie Garden Café and Tearoom welcomes walkers. It is a place of some ancient charm being located in the old stables. It is open 10-5pm. In winter it is closed on Mondays. Ring the day before if you are a large group, 01721 722 807

THE WALK

NB Some tracks have name boards like those in city streets. However the tracks are not tarmac.

1   2.2km; 130m; 46'

A footbridge enters the car park. Locate it. It is your return route. From the car park take the track beside the toilet block, Kirkburn Road, heading S beside the Kirk Burn. Almost immediately take a path going off over another footbridge to the L, E. Where the path divides take the right hand lane since it is not used by horses so much. Ignoring any paths off to the L climb up hill and down again to meet a broader track about 1.9km, 30', later.
GR NT2945 365   2.2km; 130m; 46'

15

Short Version saving about 1hr.

1.5km; 160m; 40'

If the weather is really bad turn L uphill on the broad track. At each junction keep heading S-ish. After about 1km you will start to curve round to the E and exit the forest 500m later. Here you rejoin the longer version at beginning of Leg 6.
GR NT3015 365

Longer Version.

2   1.1km; 80m; 25'

In acceptable weather turn R downhill on the broad track for a few metres to intersect the track by the Kirk Burn. Turn L, SW-ish on it. About 500m later turn L to leave this track and cross the stream, now called the Highlandshiels Burn, by a footbridge. Follow the path uphill through a tunnel of trees. At a junction keep R, SE-ish and continue to ascend for perhaps 350m to come to a wide junction.
GR NT2939 3585   3.3km; 210m; 1h11'

Robin

3   0.7km; 10m; 11'

Turn sharp R, NW-ish, on a broad track. Contour on this as it swings round to head roughly S. Do not go up or down from this as it narrows to a mini path just after a discontinuity.
GR NT289 3555   4km; 220m; 1h22'

4   1km; 40m; 19'

Your path is really a firebreak. Your next obstacle is a stream crossing. The banks are steep so go with care. Regain the path on the southern side. Soon it narrows again to a mini path and 300m later exits the forest.
GR NT285 3475   5km; 260m; 1h41'

5   2.3km; 125m; 48'

Turn L, SE-ish on the forest-side path to climb up to a gate. Do NOT go through, inviting though it may seem. Stick to the forest edge on your left. Follow it over Little Craigie Side, across Orchard Rig, over Beards Hill and Grieston Hill all the while making sure to enjoy the panoramas all around. Descend to a meeting of tracks and a sharp bend in the forest edge. This is where the Short Version joins.
GR NT3015 365   7.3km; 385m; 2h29'

6   1.3km; 10m; 21'

The track, now Wallace Hill Road, ascends just W of N and then descends to a fork. Take the L hand one and

Castle Knowe fort dates from about 1000BC. It was built on the walls of a much older site, possibly 2000BC. It continued to be used even after the Roman invasion. Their camp was in the valley below. Many of the stones have been reused in modern times to make a sheep fank.

This pele tower was built in the 16ᵗʰ century. It would have been a well- fortified home. Today its ruin makes a hibernating roost for pipistrelle and soprano pipistrelle bats. Do not disturb them.

Pele Tower

ascend into the forest area again leaving the moorland behind you. GR NT3025 3557
This track contours NE on the side of Wallace Hill. It then descends rapidly to join Wallace Hill Road again. Turn L, NW-ish.
GR NT3088 3661   8.6km; 395m; 2h50'

7   1.5km; 50m; 28'
The track goes round a wide S-shaped bend. After 1.2km, 15'-20', from joining Wallace Hill Road turn L on Castleknowe South Road. Leave it 100m later on a small path. After about 50m again turn R off it. Follow up the hillside to Castle Knowe fort. Enjoy the views.
GR NT302 3727   10.1km; 445m; 3h18'

8   0.8km; 0m; 12'
Enter the walled area and cross it to where the wall is partially broken down in the NE corner. You could also circumnavigate outside round the walled area going clockwise to reach the same point. Pick your way gingerly down over the moss-covered foundation stones of the fort. Carefully descend the steep slope through the trees heading E of N to Castleknowe Road, 150m below. Turn L, NW-ish on it. About 750m, 11' later turn R, NE on a path which leads down to the ruin of a pele tower.
GR NT3008 379   10.9km; 445m; 3h30'

9   0.7km; 40m; 15'
Continue to descend on the path, heading N to join a road serving some local houses. Turn L, N-ish on it. Ahead on the L is the entrance to a house. Go past it round a barrier on to a track which curves round W-ish and up to join Kirkburn Upper Road.
GR NT299 386   11.6km; 485m; 3h45'

10   1km; 0m; 15'
500m later where Kirkburn Upper Road turns S find, on your R, a small path zigzagging W rapidly down through the trees to cross the Kirk Burn and return you to your car.
                 12.6km; 485m; 4h

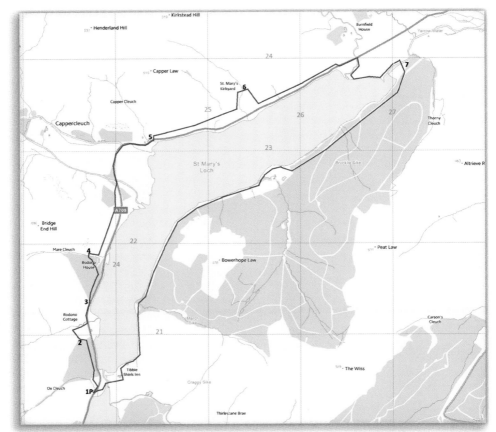

Not to scale

18

3 • CIRCUIT OF St MARY'S LOCH

A low level walk with some difficult fences and terrain. Interesting old kirkyard.

MAP OS Explorer **330** Moffat & St Mary's Loch

Distance 13.1km
Ascent 150m
Walking time 3h34'
Allow 4h30' If you leave Edinburgh at 9am you should finish around 3pm. This is useful information for the café.
Highest elevation 310m

PARK at Glen Café where St Mary's Loch joins Loch of the Lowes GR NT238 205; TD7 5LH.

TO GET THERE Take the A703 S to Peebles. Turn L on to the A72 to Innerleithen. Shortly after you enter the village turn right on to the B709 Traquair Road. 7mls later at the crossroads in the Yarrow valley at The Gordon Arms Hotel turn right on to the A708. Drive past St Mary's Loch to find the parking place GR NT238 205, TD7 5LH.

CAFÉ For post walk coffee let the Glen Café know the day before that you are coming and how many in the party. They are very helpful. Tel No. 01750 42241. In the winter they are open only on Fridays, Saturdays and Sundays. In any case during the winter months there are not enough daylight hours to do the walk in comfort so they should be open when you need them.

TOILETS are situated above the southern end of the car park and seem to be open year round.

Bufftailed bumble bee on hawkweed

The Ettrick Shepherd, born hereabouts in 1770, was one James Hogg, an associate of Sir Walter Scott. He wrote great volumes of poetry in the popular romantic style with some fine passages.

THE WALK

1   700m; 30m; 14'
Up behind the café at the north end is a statue of the Ettrick Shepherd. There is also a sheep fank which has several interesting information boards inside. Walkers can assemble here to read the information.
Just behind the statue of the Ettrick Shepherd the telephone line cuts a swathe through the forest making a convenient, if muddy, track to follow. Emerging from the trees you meet a fence. Turn uphill along this fence to find a rickety gate a few metres up. Pass through it.
GR NT236 2095   0.7km; 30m; 14'

2 450m; 0m; 7'

You find yourself between a fence and an old stone wall. Below you, across a field, is Rodondo Cottage where they train sheepdogs. You circumnavigate their field by following the stone wall right round and down to the road. Keep the wall on your right. En route you have to pass through a gate and skirt along the stream. Turn left, N, on the road to cross the stream and find a small lay-by.

GR NT237 212   1.15km; 30m; 21'

3 650m; 40m; 14'

On the north side of this layby find a somewhat overgrown track which leads gradually up through a rickety gate to enter the forest and reveal a beautiful woodland ride with deciduous trees to the right and conifers to the left. This ride leads to a gate with 'Keepout' notices. It marks the grounds of Rodondo House. Keep to the left of the gate and proceed over rough terrain along the forest edge keeping the fence on your right. Just before you reach a stream at the end of the forest you will find a track cut up through the bracken to the underground watertank of Rodondo marked by a manhole cover. Walk past this to the stream where you can step across and clamber up the steep bank opposite. You are met with a fence which you must climb – a somewhat athletic performance.

GR NT237 219   1.80km; 70m; 35'

St Mary's Kirkyard

4 1.9km; 10m; 30'

Follow a narrow track steeply down beside the stream until you are level with the house. Look for a broad track to the L, N and follow it through the bracken roughly parallel to the road. Keep fairly low down but skirting boggy areas by finding tracks above them. After about 600m, 9' or 10', you will see a gate exiting to the road. Do not take it but pass well above it to avoid the soggy ground. Passing a fenced area of trees on your left descend to the next gate, marked at the time of writing with a red and yellow marker pole. On the road turn L to cross the Megget Water. Walk round the bend of the road to pass Cappercleuch. Take the signposted "Ring o' the Loch" path on to the hillside.

GR NT244 231   3.7km; 80m; 1h05'

5 1.3km; 60m; 26'

Follow the broad track E for about a kilometre. On a clear day you will see a white house on the other side of the Loch. This and a sign post to St Mary's Kirkyard will alert

The remains of St Mary's Kirk are in the NW corner of the graveyard under the grassy mound. It was burnt in 1557 in an interfamily feud. On the last Sunday of July there is a 'blanket' service here in memory of the fact that Covenanters often had a blanket as their only shelter.

Tibbie Shiels was born in 1782. Before her marriage she worked for the parents of James Hogg, the Ettrick Shepherd. At the age of 41 she was left with 6 children, the widow of a molecatcher. To make a livelihood she made wayfarers welcome, if not comfortable - her beds were of a size to challenge airport sleeping pods! Wordsworth was one of the famous who stayed with her. Tibbie died at the age of 95.

you that it will soon be time to turn up, N, along the west side of a deep gully on a broad grassy track. GR NT253 234. This track leads across the stream at the top of the gully. Before you are the ruins of the Kirkyard. Take time to read the information board with its tales of black deeds. The writings on the grave stones, especially one just below the ruined mausoleum, tell poignant family stories.
GR NT254 236   5km; 140m; 1h31'

6   2.1km; 0m; 32'

After spending some time viewing the stones find a wooden footbridge to the South East of the kirkyard across the stream. Follow the grassy path on the other side directly down almost to the road where you will find a broad grass track heading NE-ish parallel to the road again. If there are cattle around, this section can be quite muddy and you may need to weave your way to find the easiest passage to a metal gate about a kilometre ahead. Go through on to the road and across. Pick up the Ring O' the Loch signs and follow them down to the water and L along the shore to the bridge. Now you have joined the Southern Upland Way leading you across the Yarrow Water.
GR NT271 238   7.1km; 140m; 2h03'

7   6km; 10m; 1h31'

On the S coast of the loch follow the SUW signs, more or less along the shore. Near the end of the loch you will see the boat club and beyond it Tibbie Shiels Inn.
On reaching the road turn R to leave the SUW. Cross the bridge. Immediately beyond the bridge you can take a steep little path down on your L. Cross the large car park diagonally to the road, your car and a welcome little something in the café.

13.1km; 150m; 3h34'

Broch remains

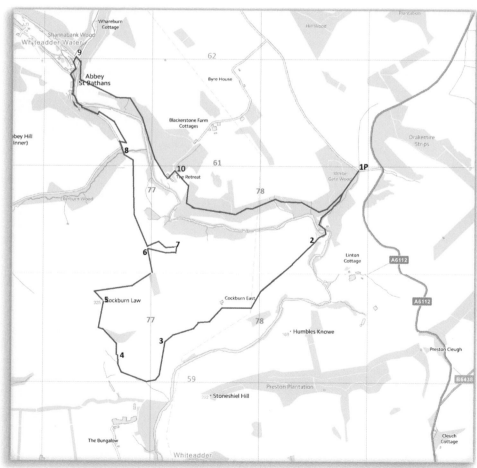

Not to scale

4 • COCKBURN LAW and EDIN'S HALL BROCH

Across a mini gorge on a swing bridge, huge prehistoric site with enigmatic broch, farmland, carpets of wild flowers, hill top views and a forest walk by the Whiteadder Water.

Pansy

WE SAW in April of a warm spring: hosts of anemones, primroses, wood sorrel, celandines, violets, dog's mercury, buzzard, sky larks, yellowhammer.

MAP OS Explorer **346** Berwick-upon-Tweed

Distance 12km
Ascent 325m
Walking Time 3h35'
Allow 4h35'
Highest Elevation 345m

PARK In the Edin's Hall Broch parking lay-by on the unclassified road at GR NT789 609

TO GET THERE Take the A1 south to Grantshouse. Turn R, SW-ish, on to the A6112 signposted Duns. About 3mls later turn R on to the unclassified road signposted Edin's Hall Broch. Park at the bottom of the hill in the lay-by.

TOILETS Convenience trees in the wood!

CAFÉ Store, Belhaven Fruit Farm 01368 860 573. EH42 1RG. GR NT651 776. To get there drive back on the A1 towards Edinburgh. There are several roundabouts serving Dunbar. You want the second one. The café is the 4th exit of the roundabout. It is signposted as a dead end.

THE WALK

1   **1km; 15m; 16'**
Walk on the track heading SW beside the burn. At the first intersection keep L. (You will return along the right hand track at the end of the walk.) Continue to follow the main track as it curves round to the left - the car route goes ahead down to ford the river. You stay on the track to cross a beautiful suspension bridge over a delightful mini gorge, Strait Leap, in the Whiteadder Water. Pass a house, Elba, on your left and go ahead up some steps on a path through the bushes. Go through a gate and into a field. Leave the path here and begin to clamber up through the lower blackthorn trees. Almost immediately

23

watch for a track going off to your left through the
blackthorns. Turn L along it to reach the open field above.
GR NT7857 6038   1km; 15m; 16'

2   1.8km; 60m; 33'
Walk just W of S diagonally up across the field. Pick up a
path which contours round the hill and leads to the gate
into the next field. Now a track, it will carry you through
this field and another one. Next you will pass the deserted
Cockburn East farm. Continue along the track as it goes
through the next gateway where another track drops
down to the riverside. Ignore it but it acts as a reassuring
marker.
GR NT772 5934   2.8km; 75m; 49'

3   0.9km; 65m; 20'
On rounding the next shoulder you will find a stream
crossing your path. Leave the track here and go R,
NW-ish upstream. Stay close to the stream to avoid
any crops. Where the stream branches take the R, NW
branch. As you climb you meet a wall. Turn N, uphill with
it to a gate. Go through.
GR NT7667 5925   3.7km; 140m; 1h09'

4   0.7km; 105m; 21'
Follow the right hand boundary round to the N, upper,
side of the field and on to find a gate beyond the trees.
Go through and climb Cockburn Law. Near the top
watch for a badger latrine – holes scooped in the hard
ground and filled with badger poo. You can see the
beetle wings shining in it!
GR NT7657 5975   4.4km; 245m; 1h30'

5   1km; 0m; 15'
Leave the trig point heading just W of N to cross the
ramparts and find a track zigzagging down in an E-ish
direction. On the flatter land it meets another track.
Cross this track and head generally NE-ish through the
whinny countryside to meet a fence round a field. Turn L,
N with it to a stile*. A path coming from your L joins here.
Don't take it now but it will be your exit route after your
visit to Edin's Hall Broch.
GR NT7695 6034   5.4km; 245m; 1h45'

6   0.3km; 10m; 6'
Cross the stile and head across the field maintaining your
height to reach a fence. Follow the fence on in the same
direction to a gate and stile into the huge prehistoric
settlement with its enormous broch. Take time to explore

Blackthorn

*The fort on Cockburn Law
probably predates Edin's
Hall Broch settlement below.
The natural defences of the
hill top were augmented
by earth and stone banks.
There were several buildings
inside and possibly a cairn.
To the south you can see the
Cheviots and to the north the
Lammermuirs.*

the site. There are several interpretation boards to help.
GR NT772 603   5.7km; 255m; 1h51'

It appears that on this prehistoric site there are three distinct phases of occupation.
a. *The first has the usual construction of a very large hill fort which dates from the pre Roman Iron Age - 200 or 100BC.*
b. *The broch, a double walled empty tower with living quarters between the walls, dates from the period between the Roman invasions – 100-200AD. Brochs are uniquely Scottish but are usually found in the west and north including the islands. This example is very large and may have been more of a status symbol than a place of refuge. The wealth of the owners may have been related to the mining of copper nearby. Heavy copper jewellery was very popular at this time throughout Scotland.*
c. *The third period of occupation is an undefended village of stone huts which overlies the earlier constructions. It is thought to have been constructed in the Pax Romana interval. The local Votadini and the Romans were quite pally.*

7   1.3km; 0m; 20'
Exit the site by the W gate and follow the path over the stile. Turn L, SW to climb up to the stile* you crossed before your visit, mentioned at the end of Leg 5. Turn R to follow the path N and gradually descend as you round the bracken covered hillside ahead. Ignore paths which take you uphill or sharply down. Finally you gradually descend to the Eller Burn and cross it on a footbridge.
GR NT7672 611   7km; 255m; 2h11'

8   1.2km; 20m; 20'
Ascend the steep steps opposite to take you on to the public road at 'Toot Corner'. Turn right. About 100m down enter the field on your right, animals permitting, and walk through it parallel to the road. (If there are cows in the field just stay on the road). Leave it where the woodland starts and continue to walk downhill on the road. Beyond the crash barrier on the right side of the road turn down some steps and across a bridge to a riverside path, in places little used - you may have to wade through vegetation. This returns you to the road, opposite a sawmill. Walk along the road for maybe 150m. Find a house on your right. Turn R just before it. Just before you reach the river veer L across the open area to pass a Southern Upland Way hut. Beside the fish farm turn R to cross the river on a high footbridge. Pause to enjoy the views.
GR NT763 620   8.2km; 275m; 2h31'

9   1.5km; 25m; 26'
Once across the footbridge turn R and cross the road. Opposite find a woodland path. Follow this up and down through whin to reach a broad track. Turn L uphill for about 200 metres almost to the bend in the track. Here turn R on a path through the woods. Follow this, parallel

to the river, up and down, through gates to reach a field below Retreat House, presently for hire as a holiday cottage. When you pass the first buildings turn L up some steps set in the little ha-ha. Pass between the buildings and on to the approach road. Go up the access road for perhaps 50m and turn R across a bridge.
GR NT7727 6091   9.7km; 300m; 2h57'

Retreat House, its walled garden and sundial are A listed. It was built as a hunting lodge by the Earl of Wemyss around 1780. It has some unusual features – octagonal rooms and undulating ceilings (intentional!).

10 2.3km; 25m; 38'

Ascend on a track between fields leading into the woods beyond. Follow this back, always heading E-ish and maintaining your approximate height, through the woodland to finally merge with your outward route. Turn L to return to your car.

12km; 325m; 3h35'

Retreat House

Strait Gorge

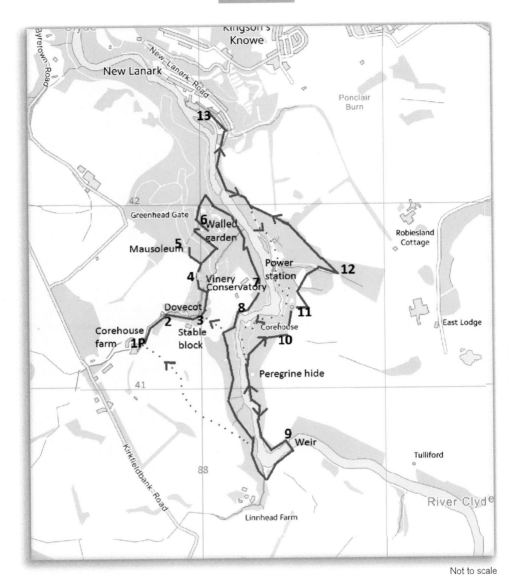

Not to scale

5 • COREHOUSE
and the FALLS of CLYDE

Walking through a World Heritage site including the remains of two great estates. Possible sightings of nesting peregrines in spring. A good wet weather walk especially following days of heavy rain when the falls will be at their thundering best.

kingfisher

WE SAW in December: heron, jay, raven. You might be lucky enough to see polecat, otter, kingfisher.

MAP OS Explorer **335** Lanark & Tinto Hills

Distance 11.1km
Ascent 395m
Walking Time 3h27'
Allow 4h30'
Highest elevation 190m

PARK For one or two cars: Entrance to Falls of Clyde Nature Reserve on Corehouse Drive. GR NS878 414.
For more than 2 cars: Corehouse Farm backyard on Corehouse Drive ML11 9TQ; GR NS876 4125. Ring the farmer to get permission to park: 01555 661 377

TO GET THERE Take the A70 S to Carnwath. Turn R on the A70. Pass Carstairs and about 1 mile further turn L still on A70. At Ravenstruther veer R on to the A743 into Lanark. In Lanark merge R on to A73. Drive through town. As road descends veer L on to A72 towards Hamilton. Cross the bridge and immediately L on to Kirkfield Rd. 500m later go L on to Byreton Rd. About 1ml later where road bends rightangled R go straight ahead on an unmetalled track which becomes Corehouse Drive. The small area of parking for the Reserve is opposite some cottages beside their bins. For more parking go 200m further, now on tarmac, to Corehouse Farm on the right. Ask permission to park. Opposite is a signpost to Bonnington Linn. This may be your return route.

TOILETS None

CAFÉ In New Lanark half way through the walk. Remember to carry your money with you.

THE WALK

1 0.2km; 0m; 3'

If you parked at the farm follow the tarmac road back
N-ish, the way you came. Notice the stone Cold House
on your right. After about 200m find the entrance to
Falls of Clyde Nature Reserve on your R. Go through the
gateway on the broad drive.

GR NS878 414   0.2km; 0m; 3'

2 0.2km; 0m; 3'

As you walk, on your right, you will see the listed stable
block. It was constructed in the early nineteenth century
at the same time as the present Corehouse mansion.
It is private. Continue down the drive for about 100m
to find a path joining from your R, E. This may be your
return route; don't take it now. Notice a gate on your
R. Immediately opposite look carefully for the ruined
dovecot partially obscured by the vegetation on your left.
Probably built in the 18th century, it predates the present
mansion. It is listed as an early example of a rectangular
dovecot. From here on through the grounds you need
to exercise your imagination by stripping out almost
all the trees and undergrowth to envisage the original
landscaped gardens. This whole area was designed,
possibly by the Landseer brothers, Charles and Edwin,
to be "pleasure grounds" planted with flowers. Walkways
criss-crossed the streams with views across the valley to
the Bonnington Estate.

GR NS8805 4139   0.4km; 0m; 6'

3 0.2km; 5m; 4'

Continue for perhaps another 100m to find a faint path
going off on your L, W. Take this across the little stream.
Do not be dismayed if you spot a notice telling you you
need permission to walk here. The law, Right to Roam,
gives you that permission. On your R you will find the
listed Conservatory which is unusual in being made of
stone. Contemporary ones were usually wood or metal. A
few steps further brings you to the remains of the vinery.
The low wall at the front would have been the footing for
the glass walls, now all gone. On the other side of the tall
wall you will see where another roof joined it. This would
have been the stove house providing heat for the vinery
and the Conservatory below.

GR NS880 415   0.6km; 5m; 10'

4 0.3km; 0m; 4'

Continue for some 100m on the same path but watch for

*This section of the Corehouse
estate has been gifted to the
Scottish Wildlife Trust as a
Nature Reserve. Rare and
secretive pine martens have
been seen. They are thought
to compete successfully
against the invasive grey
squirrels.*

Dovecot

Conservatory

Vinery

*After the first Lord Corehouse
completed his home he had
a stroke, in 1840. This
prompted him to construct his
mausoleum. He survived for
another 20 years.*

Mausoleum

Greenhouses

*Corehouse Mansion was
built in 1824 in the Tudor
Revival style by the architect,
Blore, who was responsible
for finishing Buckingham
Palace. It replaced a
Georgian mansion owned by
the Edmounston family. Only
2 spinster ladies survived
in that clan so the property
passed to the Cranstouns
who still own it. The title
Lord Corehouse was a legal
one.*

a lesser one going off to the L, NW-ish. The main path*
goes straight ahead. You will return to this presently. Just
now keep to the L on the small path which runs by the
side of a field at first. Keep looking into the trees to spot
the Mausoleum. A track veers off to the L to take you
there. You can peer through its slatted iron windows to
see an altar type stone inside. The building is still in use.
GR NS879 4175   0.9km; 5m; 14'

5   0.5km; 0m; 8'
Return to the main path* mentioned above. Continue
L along it crossing a major path after 100 m. Your path
bends round to the L heading downhill. You cross a
bridge and now, to your R, you should spot the remains
of the old greenhouses. Your path swings R and almost
immediately on the R at GR NS879 419 find a track
leading in to the old gardens. Immediately through
the wall you can go L to stoop through the ruined
glasshouses minding your feet on the broken glass.
Once again in your mind's eye you have to remove
the trees and undergrowth and replace them with a
great kitchen garden – peaches, grapes, pineapples
and nectarines in the glasshouses and vegetables and
orchards around you. Explore the site continuing to
descend. At the bottom of the hill turn L out through the
huge walls to join a more established path. Turn R.
GR NS881 4195   1.4km; 5m; 22'

6   0.6km; 60m; 15'
Descend to the riverside and turn upstream. Stop on the
bridge across the Corra Burn and look up the hill on your
R. You may be able to spot the remains of a set of steps
which would have been part of the pretty journey through
the extensive shrubbery of the 19th century. Soon on the
opposite bank you will see the large white building which
is the hydroelectric power station GR NS884 416. It
was built in 1920, the first commercial one in Britain.
Follow upstream and as the path continues to ascend
you will spot a sign which says 'Private path to House'.
Do not take it but a few metres further on climb up to the
edge of the trees to get a view of Corehouse Mansion.
GR NS883 4156   2km; 65m; 37'

7   0.3km; 50m; 8'
Continue upstream to reach Corra Linn Falls where the
Clyde is forced through a narrow gorge crashing down
two great steps in a roaring torrent. Take full advantage
of the outlook points to appreciate the massive power of
the falls. (See information on next page).

A few more metres brings you to Cora Castle, the home of the Bannatyne family in the 15th century. At that time they owned the estate on the other bank of the river as well.
GR NS8825 414   2.3km; 115m; 45'

8   1.2km; 35m; 22'

After all that sightseeing you can stride out now continuing upstream. You may notice the peregrine-watch hide on the other side as you go. Soon you reach the spectacular Bonnington Linn, a double fall. The spray from it, in flood conditions, creates a rain forest effect with ferns and mosses thriving. Beyond the falls is the weir where the water to drive the power station is siphoned off. Cross the footbridge. The automated mechanism for keeping the weir-water free of debris is fun to watch through a couple of sweeps, if it is working.
GR NS885 4065   3.5km; 150m; 1h07'

9   0.8km; 5m; 13'

Once across turn L, N. Soon you will reach the peregrine watch hide. This is manned 24/7 during the nesting time. The nest is on a mini ledge opposite. Round the next bend turn R, E uphill away from the water.
GR NS8827 4115   4.3km; 155m; 1h20'

10 0.5km; 50m; 13'

As the forest thins you should see, on your R, the remains of the walled garden of Bonnington House. The house was an elegant mansion which unfortunately caught fire in 1914. It was finally demolished in the 1920s. As the path ascends you will get glimpses of Lanark looking like a hill top village and of New Lanark by the waterside in the gorge. Next comes the circular tank collecting the water from Bonnington Weir before it descends through the enormous pipes to feed the power station below. Just below you is the stone building which is the remains of Bonnington Pavilion built in 1708 by Sir James Carmichael. It was fitted out with mirrors which gave observers the impression of standing under the raging torrent below. The mirrors meant elegant ladies were saved from the !unsettling! effects of viewing nature in the raw.
GR NS885 4143   4.8km; 2055m; 1h33'

11 0.7km; 50m; 15'

Return to just below the water tank and pass its lower side to enter the nearby field by a pedestrian gate. Approximately 100m along the top of the field turn L, S

Cora Falls have inspired poets and artists. Wordsworth called them "Clyde's most majestic daughter". Turner sketched them. That work is in the Tate, not in Edinburgh. Sir Walter Scott often visited as did Coleridge among many others. Wallace had one of his many caves in the cliffs. Now it's your turn to pay homage! There are many suggestions for the derivation of the name Corra or Cora. The most mundane is that it is from an ancient word meaning 'marshy place'. A more fanciful one says Cora was the daughter of Malcolm II, who founded Old Pentland Church (Walk 15). In a state of love-induced desperation she rode to her death from the cliff above. Poor horse! The castle had 4 vaulted cellars, 3 of which are still intact and which now provide a protected home for both Daubenton and natterer bats. Above the cellars was a grand hall and above that the family bedrooms. Down by the water was a corn mill.

Was it here Tennyson found inspiration to write:

"She left the web, she left the loom
She made three paces thro' the room
She saw the water-lily bloom,
She saw the helmet and the plume,
*   She look'd down to Camelot.*
Out flew the web and floated wide;
The mirror crack'd from side to side;
'The curse is come upon me,' cried
*   The Lady of Shalott"?*

and follow a narrow muddy path as it snakes down to the flatter area below. Cross this scrubby, flatter area heading E-ish again and then drop down to the remains of an old mill on the Robiesland Burn. Just downstream of the ruin a tiny bridge takes you across the stream. Climb steeply up the other bank to the roadway. Turn R, uphill. About 200m later turn L off the road on a clearly marked path.

GR NS887 416   5.5km; 215m; 1h48'

12 1.2km; 20m; 20'
Follow this track as it curves round high above the river. Soon you are joined by a track from your L. About 200m beyond this junction take a little side path on your L to take you down to the Clyde. Once there turn R and walk to New Lanark. Beyond the archway stay at the same level. Pass the water wheel and find the café on your L. Enjoy your refreshment. If time permits you might visit the excellent Scottish Wildlife Centre where you can find news of badgers, otters and other wildlife of the woods and river.

GR NS881 425   6.7km; 225m; 2h08'

13   Your return journey takes you upstream again, through the archway and along the Clyde Walkway directly to Bonnington Linn. Cross the weir and start downstream. Almost immediately follow the wide path L away from the river. Cross a burn on a bridge and continue N parallel to the Clyde for about 150m or so. Here:

EITHER 4km; 120m; 1h12'
find a faint path leaving your broader track going L, NW. Take it up out of the forest at a gate and across 2 muddy fields to your car at Corehouse Farm. If you parked at the entrance to the Nature Reserve you must turn R on the metalled road for a couple of hundred metres, past the Cold House, to your vehicle.

10.7km; 395m; 3h20'

OR 4.4km; 120m; 1h19'
if time allows use a longer but less muddy alternative: continue for about another km to the next L turn. Take this and follow it to the access road. Turn L to return to your car.

11.1km; 395m; 3h27'

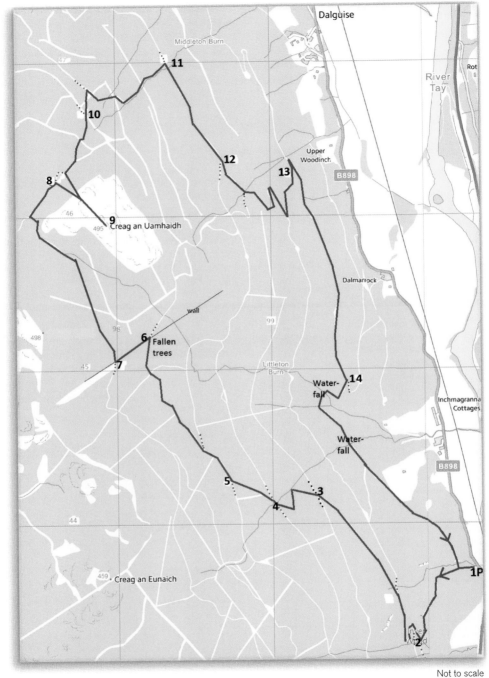

Not to scale

6 • Creag an Uamhaidh, Craigvinean Forest

The Crag of the Caves in the
Crag of the Goats Forest

A walk on and off forest trails, some broad and easy, others more overgrown. Some difficult terrain. No very steep slopes. Excellent views on a clear day.

Gossamer spider webs

'With gossamer threads the fields were laid,
Which shimmered like silk while the sunlight played.'

Cep mushroom (penny bun, boletus)

WE SAW on a misty August day: blooming heather, gossamer spider webs, self heal, spear thistle, milkwort, broom pods, rowan berries, cep mushroom (penny bun, boletus), beautiful mosses, jays and roe deer.

MAP OS Explorer **379**, Dunkeld, Aberfeldy & Glen Almond

Distance 13.35km
Ascent 480m
Walking Time 4h14'
Allow 5h
Highest elevation 495m

PARK in Craigvinean Car Park off the B898, just off the A9 N of Dunkeld.

TO GET THERE take the A9 N. About 1 mile N of Dunkeld turn L on to the B898. Car park is immediately on your L.

TOILETS None except for the convenience trees.

CAFÉ Stewart Tower Farm café and ice cream parlour. To get there drive 7.8 miles S on the A9. Turn L on to an unclassified road signed Stewart Tower Ice Cream and Bankfoot. Immediately go L and drive about 1 mile. The farm is on your R. It closes at 4.30pm. Tel 01738 710 044. Sat Nav PH1 4PJ

THE WALK

The forest has a series of broad forest tracks running roughly SE to NW. This route to the summit goes from one track to the next highest using overgrown, often steeply ascending, linking paths which can be treacherous underfoot and require more careful navigation. As you gain height you are rewarded with wonderful views.

1. **0.8km; 20m; 14'**
   Go through the gate and walk up to the corner. Take the small path to the L, W heading uphill. Ascend with it.

It flattens out and becomes a broad track heading S-ish.
400 m later reach a T junction.
GR NN9991 43220   8km; 20m; 14'

2. **1.5km; 145m; 37'**
Turn R, NW. Ignore first L. The track zigzags up to turn
N. 250m later take the L, NW fork in the track. Ascend
steadily. 0.8km, 24' later reach a junction of tracks.
GR NN9929 4418   2.3km; 165m; 51'

3. **0.4km; 55m; 13'**
Choose the somewhat overgrown track heading steeply
up in a W-ish direction. Ignoring all side shoots, ascend
in the W-ish direction straight ahead for about 150m.
Now the track turns L for some 100+m to avoid a small
gorge. Next it goes R for a similar distance to join a broad
track. Having done almost half of the day's ascent this
might be a good place to have a little refreshment to re-
energise yourself for some rough stuff ahead.
GR NN9905 4411   2.7km; 220m; 1h04'

4. **0.3km; 30m; 8'**
Turn R across a burn. About 10m beyond the stream turn
L uphill on to another grassy track with some bushes on
your R. 0.3km, 8' later emerge from the undergrowth to
reach a T junction.
GR NN9871 4428   3km; 255m; 1h12'

5. **1.15km; 20m; 19'**
Turn R, W of N. Approx. 300m later, at a junction, keep
L. Contour N for about 750m passing through an area of
wind-devastated forest. Just beyond the fallen trees you
should be able to spot an old wall visible to both the L
and R of the track.
GR NN982 452   4.15km; 275m; 1h31'

6. **0.3km; 30m; 9'**
You are going to go up across country to the next big
track by following a little path roughly parallel to the wall
keeping it on your L side. Underfoot it is treacherous
so go cautiously. Cross the boggy drain on your left on
some rough logs. Your path ascends steeply from there.
At first there is a line of discarded branches on your left.
Beyond them the path crosses some slippery embedded
branches to be closer to the wall. Make your way ahead,
beside the wall, through some tall bracken. Try to avoid
skin contact. (Bracken often harbours ticks which may
carry Lyme's disease). Beyond the bracken the path turns
away from the wall slightly to enter the forest but, once

Broom pods

Rowan berries

into the wood, continues roughly parallel. Finally, still in the woodland, the path veers R to take you triumphantly on to the next broad track.
GR NN9797 4506   4.45km; 305m; 1h40'

7. 1.5km; 85m; 32'
Turn R, N-ish. Walk up this track. It ascends steadily for just over a km, levels out and then goes down. As the descent begins the trees on your R gradually disappear to be replaced by craggy outcrops. As the mini cliffs disappear look for a moss-covered passing place on your R. Just at the beginning of it find a very small path heading across a boggy area.
GR NN976 4626   5.95km; 390m; 2h12'

Due N	Cairngorm Mountains
40°	Glenshee Mountains and Lochnagar
62°	Deuchary Hill and Loch Ordie just N of it
234°	Ben Chonzie
246°	Ben More
260°	Ben Lawers range
290°	Shiehallion
354°	Ben a Ghlo

8. 0.5km; 50m; 13'
Take this indistinct path and mind your footing as you cross some slippery branches and begin the ascent. As you climb you will notice a path* joining you from the L. This is your return route. Continue upwards over the first top and on back to the large cairn on Creag an Uamhaidh. Enjoy the views.
GR NN980 460   6.45km; 440m; 2h25'

9. 0.9km; 10m; 15'
Leave back the way you came, roughly NW. Use the same route for most of the way. At the fork take the R path* down to the broad forest track again. Turn R, NE-ish. Follow this track down to join a broader track at a U bend.
GR NN978 4665   7.35km; 450m; 2h40'

Roe deer

The next 3 legs zigzag you down to a low level track. The intervening distances and times can be crucial in helping you find the route. You won't always be on the most frequented ways. GRs can reassure you.

10. 0.75km; 0m; 12'

Go ahead, N, using the R track. 150m later at a T junction turn R, SE-ish. Zigzag down about 600m to another T junction.
GR NN9831 4700   8.1km; 450m; 2h52'

11. 0.6km; 10m; 9'

Turn R, SE-ish again. 0.6km, 9' later just as the track begins to climb again, look for a not-very-obvious wide grassy path on your L, 160°. There may be a marker post by it.
GR NN987 464   8.7km; 460m; 3h01'

12. 0.95km; 0m; 15'

Take the broad grassy path. 0.4km later at the next junction keep L again, E-ish. Zigzag down for about 550m to a T junction.
GR NN991 460   9.65km; 460m; 3h16'

13. 1.8km; 10m; 28'

Turn L, N. 400m later turn sharp R, SE-ish. Walk on this broad track for 1.4km, some 20'. Now on your R find a grassy track heading just W of S.
GR NN9948 449   11.45km; 470m; 3h44'

14. 1.9km; 10m; 30'

Take the grassy track. Follow it past a couple of pretty waterfalls all the way back to the cars.
         13.35km; 480m; 4h14'

7 • CULTER FELL

At 748m, just short of a Corbett, the fourth highest hill in the Borders being topped by Broad Law, White Coomb and Hart Fell. This ascent is from the Broughton side.

Very steep ascents and descents and some rough terrain but the views are spectacular. Do it on a clear day.

Raven ©Safari

WE SAW in July: raven, kestrel, eyebright, red rattle, butterwort, nearly ripe cloudberries.

MAP OS Explorer **336** Biggar & Broughton Culter Fell & Dollar Law

Distance 9km
Ascent 654m
Walking Time 3h25'
Allow 4h30'
Highest elevation 748m

PARK at Glenkirk GR NT0793 294

TO GET THERE travel south on the A701, Moffat road. 4 miles beyond Leadburn note Whitmuir Organic Centre on your left. This is the coffee venue for afterwards. Continue past Broughton (about 25miles south of Edinburgh). Just over a mile further take the minor road on the R signed Glenholm. Follow this narrowing road past Glenholm. At the fork keep L. Do not cross the burn but continue past the farm of Glencotho with its sheep dogs to Glenkirk. A board warns you to drive no further. Park on the grass verge making sure to cause no obstruction.

TOILETS None

CAFÉ Whitmuir Organic Centre on the A701 a couple of miles north of Romannobridge and just beyond some speed tracks across the road.

THE WALK

1   **0.5km; 70m; 15'**
    From the car park you can't see Coulter Fell. It is behind the green Congrie Hill but you can see Chapelgill to the NW which you will climb on the way.
    Go past the end of the wall and immediately turn R, W-ish. Pass Glenkirk house and go L and then R past

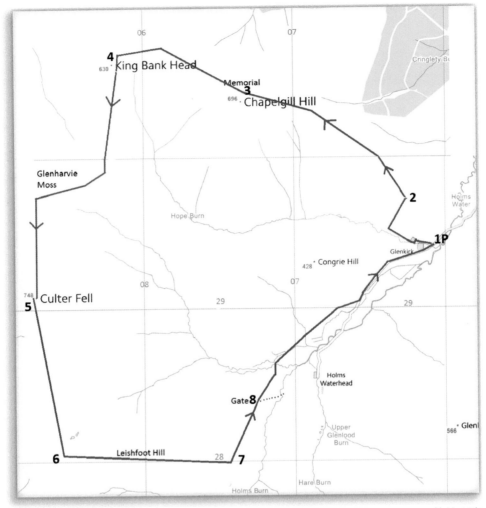

Not to scale

the sheds to reach a gateway on to the hill. Leave the broad track, following instead a fainter path more or less parallel to the burn. When you reach the fence go R and ascend steeply with it. At the top of the slope you will find a fenced-in area on your R. Once in line with it go through the fence on your L on to the open hill.
GR NT077 297   0.5km; 70m; 15'

2   1.3km; 426m; 1h03'
Once through the fence walk on a bearing of about 325° continue up to a fence. Continue uphill, with the fence as it climbs the steep side of Chapelgill. At the top you will find a small memorial cairn to someone called James King with a plaque on the neighbouring fence post. This fence is not marked on older OS maps.
GR NT067 3038   2.5km; 446m; 1h23'

3   1km; 10m; 16'
Follow the fence in a generally westerly direction. Wiggle to avoid the wettest areas. Looking SW across the valley of the Hope Burn you will see the Glenharvie ridge and, towering above it, Culter Fell.
Watch for the large crinkly, lobed leaves of cloudberries. They have big white flowers leading to strawberry-like red berries which are orange when ripe. The whole plant seems exotic for such a habitat.
Ahead of you, you will see the transverse fence called Dun Knees (not prophetic we hope). Use the quad bike track to cut down and across to join it. The grid reference is approximate depending on exactly where you join the fence. (This will be your new handrail and part way down Culter Fell).
GR NT059 306   2.9km; 456m; 1h34'

4   2km; 168m; 47'.
Follow the track roughly paralleling the fence in a southerly direction slightly up and then down towards King Bank Head and the peat hags of Glenharvie Moss. Your track bypasses them by leaving the fence and skirting round the boggy area, keeping it on your right. Beyond the sog, rejoin the fence and settle in for the slog up to the trig point of Coulter Fell. The views make it worthwhile.
GR NT053 291   4.9km; 624m; 2h21'

5   1km; 0m; 15'
It is probably worth descending on the R, W side of the fence where there is a bit of a path and less vegetation – more tundra like.
During your descent you will see below you to the W the star-shaped reservoir, Culter Waterhead.

On a very clear day away to the N are the Grampians.

11°	*West Lomond Hill*
24°	*Scald Law and the Pentlands*
27°	*Broughton Heights*
45°	*Moorfoots beyond Peebles*
97°	*Dollar Law*
142°	*White Coomb above the Grey Mare's Tail*
150°	*Tala Reservoir*
	Away to the S is the Lake District
223°	*Green Lowther with its masts near Wanlockhead*
233°	*Corserine in the Galloway Hills*
270°	*Goat Fell on Arran*
298°	*Tinto*
350°	*Ben Cleuch and the Ochils*

Coulter Waterhead

About 600m down ignore a gate and a fence going off to the east on your left. Continue down to a soggy area. Get across it as you can and just before the col find a second fence going off on your left. This one is for you. Climb over to it.
GR NT055 281   6.9km; 624m; 2h36'

Carniverous Butterwort

6   1km;10m; 16'
Follow this fence on its N side as it descends Leishfoot Hill. Again, pass the first fence going off on the left, N-ish, and pick up the track beyond the second fence.
GR NT065 280   6.9km; 634m; 2h52'

7   0.4km; 0m; 6'
You will follow this only through this field as it sweeps diagonally down and across to a gateway.
On leaving the field you will find a gate immediately on your L. Leave the track and go through the gate. Look ahead along the valley to see the house called Glenkirk and your car in the distance. Holms Waterhead is the house nearby on your R at the top of the valley.
GR NT0679 2832   7.3km; 634m; 2h58'

8   1.7km; 20m; 27'
Make your way along the Holms valley past a sheep fold made of metal and across a burn. Cross another burn on a bridge this time and go into the next field. Cross it diagonally. Exit at the gate to join the main stony track leading back to your car.
                               9.0km; 654m; 3h25'

Along this damp track look for the carnivorous butterwort. The leaves look like pale green stars. They are covered with sticky glands which can emit juices to digest trapped insects which are an important source of extra nitrogen for the plant. In late spring or summer they bear a strikingly beautiful blue trumpet on a longish stalk.

8 • Dunsyre Hills

A walk over the last range of the Pentlands visiting the prehistoric settlement on Dunsyre Hill and passing Oaken Bush where the Covenanter died. Do it on a clear day to help navigation.

WE SAW in February: 6 buzzards, 2 ravens and beautiful mosses.

MAP OS Explorer **344** Pentland Hills, Penicuik and West Linton

Distance: 10.45 km
Ascent: 303m
Walking Time 3h14'
Allow 4h30'
Highest elevation 450m

PARK at Easton Farm GR NT0845 492

TO GET THERE take the A702 S for some 20mls. Just beyond the sign for Dolphinton turn R indicated Dunsyre and Garvald. Follow the Dunsyre signs R and R again. Just before the village the road kinks R through the old railway. Just beyond, turn R on an unclassified road signed Dunsyre Mains. Drive just over a mile to the end of the metalled road. Turn L into Easton Farm access track. At the farm entrance turn R towards the house and immediately L into an area near the grain silo and old caravan. Park in this old courtyard. This is courtesy of the very helpful farmer.

TOILETS None.

CAFÉ Cobbs at Craigdon, 44 Biggar Road, open 9am to 6pm. Telephone 07930 564574 in advance if you are a large group.

Cultivation terraces were an early farming technique dating from the Bronze Age but lasting through mediaeval times in Scotland. Modern vineyards use the same technique. The terraces were often on steep land above the marsh and woodland below. They were on S facing slopes warmed by the sun and well drained. They would initially have been laboriously hewn out with primitive tools.

THE WALK

1   **1km; 10m; 16'**
Leave the parking area and return to the access track. Turn R, E and then R again N to walk through the farmyard. Leave it by the double gate. Follow the broad track for about 100m. Where it turns sharply R go straight ahead into a field. Follow the track as it curves L to be heading SW-ish. Go through the next 2 fields with some woodland on your L. Stop level with the end of the woodland. Ahead across the next field you can see extensive cultivation terraces.
GR NT0775 4912   1km; 10m; 16'

43

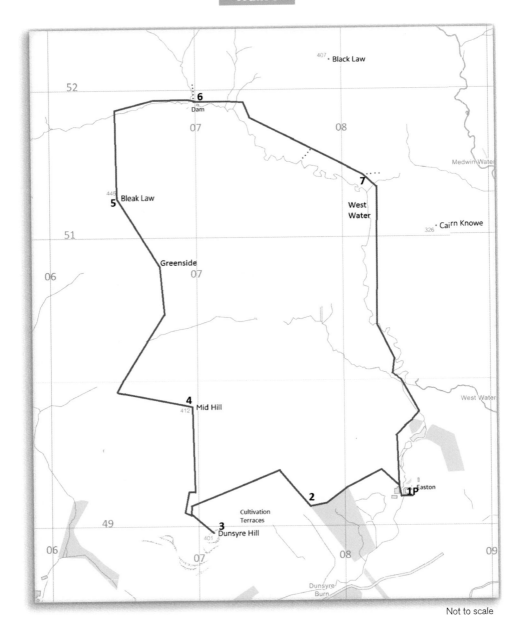

Not to scale

20°	Scald Law
90°	Wether Law
150°	Broughton Heights
180°	Culter Fell
230°	Tinto

Bugle

2   1.3km; 141m; 34'

Go through the gate immediately in front of you. Turn R and ascend NW-ish beside a drainage ditch. Near the top of the field turn L, NW-ish following the ditch. Go through an old fence and continue to the skyline where you reach a gate*. Note it but don't go through now – you will return to it. Make your way SE-ish across the open land to ascend to the cairn and prehistoric settlement at the summit. Enjoy the views.
GP NT0714895   2.3km; 151m; 50'

3   1.1km; 32m; 20'

Look along a bearing of 348° to identify Mid Hill, your next destination. Leave the cairn by your ascent route, ie in a W-ish and then NW-ish direction. Other descents are dangerously steep. Go through the gateway* mentioned in Leg 1. Once through the gate follow the wall on your R as it curves round to meet a fence. Cross the fence where it meets the wall. Be careful of loose stones. Now on the open moorland head due N-ish to reach the summit of Mid Hill.
GR NT 070 498   3.4km; 183m; 1h10'

4   2km; 115m; 42'

Look along a bearing of 348° to identify the summit of Greenside and beyond it the twin towers of Bleak Law. Your first port of call is Greenside. It is easiest to reach it by descending W-ish from Mid Hill to pick up a path which takes you roughly in your required direction. Continue to pick your best way to reach the summit of Greenside, GR NT067 508, and then the cairns of Bleak Law.
GR NT065 5125   5.4km; 298m; 1h52'

5   1.1km; 0m; 17'

Your next destination is a dam below in the valley on a bearing of 27°. However, to avoid the steepest slopes, it is best to descend N-ish to the stream. Cross it where you can and follow it E to the dam. Somewhere near here is Oaken Bush where the Covenantor died. He is buried on Black Law which rises above the dam to the NE. (See walk 25).
GR NT070 519   6.5km; 298m; 2h09'

6   1.2km; 5m; 23'

Cross the West Water where you can and pick up the broad E/W track. Go R, E. Walk along it for over a km to the second exit which goes S to continue to follow the West Water.
GR NT081 515   7.7km; 303m; 2h32'

45

7 **2.75km; 0m; 42'**

For about 30' follow the track S along the meandering West Water crossing it twice before reaching a T junction near some woodland. Turn R, SW. Go through the gate into the field and follow the track as it meanders across the rough pasture down to Easton Farm and your car.

10.45km; 303m; 3h14'

Ragged Robin

9 • EDDLESTON CIRCULAR

A walk with a bit of everything: moorland, forest, hill, riverside, a memorial, disused railway, some prehistory and the option to visit an outdoor 3D map of Scotland – the Mapa. – on a scale of 1:10,000.

Harebell

Black Barony began as a 16th century tower house erected by the Murrays of Blackbarony. It has been added to over the centuries in a somewhat higgledly piggledly way. It was used as the Polish Higher Military School during the Second World War. General Maczek was in charge. Later when a fellow Pole, Tomasik, owned the hotel he gave the general a penthouse flat. Together, in 1975, they designed and had built the Mapa in the grounds. It was designed as a tourist attraction as well as a monument to the work of the Polish Army in defending the coast of Britain. General Maczek died in 1994 aged 102.

WE SAW in June; plover, curlew, buzzard, yellowhammer, wren, stone chat, heath bedstraw, crosswort, milkwort, flowering whin, yellow flag iris, forget-me-not, water crowfoot.

MAP OS Explorer **337**, Peebles & Innerleithen

Distance 14.9km;
Ascent 470m;
Walking Time 4h31';
Allow 5h30'
Highest elevation 427m

PARK at the Black Barony Hotel, Eddleston. EH45 8QW. GR NT2367 4726

TO GET THERE take the A703 S to Eddleston. Turn R on to Old Manse Road signposted Lyme via the Meldons. Cross the bridge and immediately turn R into the hotel driveway. Sat Nav: Lat: 55.711887 Long: -3.208812

TOILETS In the hotel.

CAFÉ The hotel will provide you with whatever level of post-walk refreshment you wish. Order at least one day ahead if you are a large group otherwise speak to reception when you arrive. Telephone: 08449 802301

THE WALK

1   1km; 50m; 20'
Leave the car park on the N side by the ascending steps. At the top turn immediately L, W. Ignore 2 branches to the L and 1 to the right. Follow the track as it curves left to cross the Dean Burn. Just beyond the bridge watch

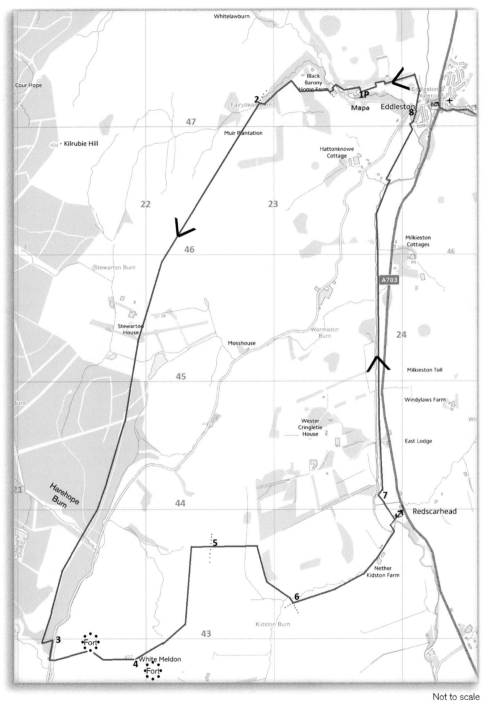

Not to scale

for a small, steeply ascending path on the R. Climb up to the broad track above. Turn R, NE-ish. Now look for a path on the L, SW-ish by a fence taking you still higher by some trees. At the top bear R, almost due N for about 75m. Stay on the path as it curves round L, SW-ish again. After all the zigzagging it is a relief to go straight for a bit through a gate, under some lovely old native woodland and finally merge with the N/S Drove Road at:
GR NT2286 4715   1km; 50m; 20'

2   4.9km; 60m; 1h19'

Now you can stride out S across moorland, through fields and finally into forest. Ignore all tracks or paths that deviate from the main S-ish direction. You are going to have to find a faint track off to the L. The trigger to start being aware is when you cross the Harehope Burn on a little footbridge. Beyond, go through a gate and across a crossroads. The stony track ascends for a short distance and then descends. Pass through a gateway. About 50m beyond this gateway and about 20m before the stony track does a sharp R bend, find a little path descending on the L. Zig zag down to the road.
GR NT2127 4295   5.9km; 110m; 1h39'

3   1.1km; 230m; 40'

Turn R, S again. Walk to the parking area beside the toilet block. Opposite cross the fence and find a bridge across the Meldon Burn. Once on the other side begin the steep ascent. Some 100m up notice a rock outcropping in the pathway. Just beyond there is a fork. Take the lesser used path on the L which leads you up into a considerable fort – one of many in this area, which must have been very populated in prehistoric times. Leave the fort by crossing its eastern defences. Turn S for a few metres to join the ascent route. Keep heading up, overall eastwards, but taking any routes which help you to avoid the heather. Reach first a cairn and then the trig point on White Meldon. You are in the middle of a very large fort.
GR NT2193 4283   7km; 340m; 2h19''

4   1.5km; 20m; 25'

Descend in a generally NE-ish direction to reach traces of another fort and settlement beside a wall. Follow this boundary N to meet a transverse boundary. Go through the gate. Turn R, E. Follow the wall on your right down the field to reach a N/S track, the access route to Upper Kidston.
GR NT226 4369   8.5km; 360m; 2h44

Meadow Brown

The White Meldon Iron Age fort is the largest in the area. At its height it had 3 defensive stone walls extending the natural defences offered by its position. It enclosed 8 acres and had at least 28 ring groove houses.

49

5   0.9km; 20m; 16'

Cross the track and find an arrowed path going downhill and then up to the SE corner of the field. Turn R, S through a gate. Turn L for a few steps to meet a N/S path running past a belt of trees. Turn R to follow the path. Continue with it through whin and across a stream with a convenient walkers' bridge. About 50m up from the bridge leave the path by turning L, NE-ish through a gate. GR NT2312 4324   9.4km; 380m; 3h

Ragwort

6   1.6km; 10m; 24'

Follow the pleasant grassy track down past Nether Kidston on your right and across the Eddleston Water on a bridge. Pass a couple of houses as you walk up to the A703 and turn L, N on the footpath. On the left you will find the house Redscarhead with a memorial wall facing N. You can go down through their gateway and into the little memorial area through a tiny gate. Here, safe from the busy road, you can sit to study the wall in peace.

The memorial commerates George Meikle Kemp, 1795-1844, a self-taught Scottish architect who started his working life as a carpenter apprenticed to Andrew Noble in this house. He is best known for the Scott Monument which was completed months after his death. His winning design was strongly influenced by the style of Melrose Abbey. He is buried in St Cuthbert's in Edinburgh within sight of his most famous work. The 3 shields are from the L: the coat of arms of Peebles, the Scottish saltire and St Ronan of Innerleithen.

Return to the footpath beside the A703 and retrace your steps into the access road. Go into the field on your R at the first gateway. Cross diagonally to its NW corner. To avoid the horse field as much as possible do not go through the gate but instead step over the wooden pallets into the field on your L. There is a stream on your

Black Barony

Cringletie was built in 1861 to a design by David Bryce, the architect responsible for Fettes, the old Royal Infirmary, Portmore House (Walk22) and Bowhill (Walk 1).

R. Follow it for a few yards to where a bridge takes you across. Again go diagonally L to take you to the banks of the Eddleston Water. Climb the wooden barrier into the horse field. Hop across a stream and leave the horse field by the gate a few metres ahead. You are now on the remnants of the old railway line linking Edinburgh and Peebles.
GR NT239 439   11km; 390m; 3h24'

7   3km; 30m; 48'
You are going to follow the Eddleston Water N back to Eddleston. Part of the way you will be on the old railway track. Where you pass under a bridge the access route to Cringletie House Hotel is above you.

Continue N towards Eddleston. With the village in view you will find some fishermen's chalets on your L. Turn L into their access road and immediately R through a gate into a field. Walk along the bottom edge of the field to find a stile into the play park. Continue along its lower edge for some 50m to find a doorway which takes you across a bridge on to Station Lye. At the end of it and across the road find the entrance to Black Barony Hotel.
GR NT242 470   14km; 420m; 4h12'

8   0.9km; 50m; 19'
To the R, E of the Black Barony Hotel driveway find the old driveway between a house and some caravans. Go along it for some 200m to where you can look up the avenue of lime trees to the hotel. Walk up. Just before the fence at the top go R, N through the line of trees. Step across a fence to a track. Turn L to a road. Turn R on it and immediately L again through the trees on to the hotel lawn. After refreshments you may wish to see the extraordinary Maczek Mapa of Scotland in the grounds.
                                    14.9km; 470m; 4h31'

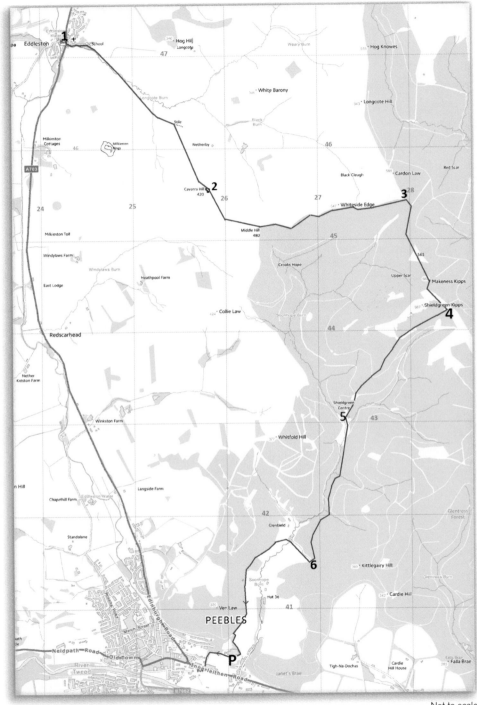

Not to scale

10 • EDDLESTON to PEEBLES
via GLENTRESS

By a stream, across fields, over hills and down through the forest to a lovely hotel. Mainly on tracks but some rough moorland as well. Linear with bus link.

Hard Going in the snow

Yarrow

Cavarra Hill may have been an outpost of the much more developed Milkieston Rings on the next hill to the NW.

MAP OS Explorer **337** Peebles & Innerleithen

Distance 10.9km
Ascent 602m
Walking Time 3h44'
Allow 4h45'
Highest elevation 587m

PARK Peebles Hydro GR NT260 405

TO GET THERE Take the A703 south to the roundabout on the outskirts of Peebles. Turn L on A72 towards Galashiels. The Hydro entrance is almost immediately on the L. Park your car up by the hotel. Return to the A72 to catch the bus to Eddleston. There is a bus stop across the road from the bottom of the Hydro avenue.

TOILETS In the Hydro.

CAFÉ If you ring ahead, 01721 720 602, the Hydro will allocate a room for a large group and serve a Borders Tea – cream scone, tea or coffee.

THE WALK

1   **1.4km; 222m; 44'**
Get off the bus at the Horseshoe Inn in Eddleston. At the south of the village find the road called Burnside which goes E through some suburban housing to pass the school. Follow the farm track beyond the school for about a kilometre, about 15'. Look for a ruined cottage on the right and just beyond it a stile. It may be signed 'Cavarra Hill'. Cross the stile and ascend S close to the wall through 2 field boundaries to emerge on the hillside. Follow the track to the summit of Cavarra with its faint remnants of a prehistoric settlement.
GR NT258 455   1.4km; 222m; 44'

2   **2.3km; 200m; 54'**
Leave the summit in a SE direction to another field boundary. Ascend E with this to Middle Hill and the

forest. Enter the woodland and follow the path E-ish between the trees and the fence along Whiteside Edge. 1.6km (24') later reach a corner in the forest where the woodland edge turns L, NW-ish. Do not go over the stile.
GR NT279 454   3.7km; 422m; 1h38'

Wheatear

3   1.5km; 110m; 34'

Turn R, SE-ish along a fence. Follow the path and fence downhill and up as they undulate over the 2 Makeness Kipps, volcanic plugs. Enjoy the views from the tops. At the bottom of the second Kipp go over a stile into an open area of rough ground. GR NT282 444. Cross this on a bearing of 142°, parallelish to the left hand forest edge and in the direction of the mast on Dunslair Heights. You will reach the beginning of the broad track which leads to the mast. Do not follow it but turn R, SW-ish down a track.
GR NT284 442   5.2km; 532m; 2h12'

4   1.9km; 0m; 28'

Follow this track, Tower Rig, in a generally SW-ish direction as it follows the side of a steep valley, crosses 2 'major' cross roads and finally curves round the remains of Shieldgreen Tower to reach a T junction with the track past Shieldgreen Centre. Turn L, SE-ish to pass the front of the centre.
GR NT273 4317.   7.1km; 532m; 2h40'

5   1.7km; 40m; 29'

Leave the grounds by the gate and, as you do so, stay on the upper path. Do not go down to cross the Soonhope Burn – not yet! Follow this track into and through the forest in a S-ish direction. Maintain this bearing avoiding turn-offs in other directions. Just over 1km, 16', later you go through a gate, ascend through a clear area and finally emerge from the woodland at the upper corner of a field.
GR NT269 415   8.8km; 572m; 3h09'

6   2.1km; 30m; 35'

Turn R to leave the broad track and descend NW-ish to cross the Soonhope Burn. At the far side go through the wooden gate on the left to ascend the hill diagonally, just S of W. This path keeps you away from Glenbeld Cottage. When you meet the main track turn L, SW-ish to parallel the Soonhope Burn downstream. After about a km, 14', as the woodland begins, take the path to the L, S, leading you down to The Hydro and your well-deserved cuppa.
GR NT260 405   10.9km; 602m; 3h44'

The Shieldgreen Tower was built for the Ingles family in the late 15th or early 16th century. It was fortified. The Shieldgreen Centre started life as a hill farm. It was acquired by the Forestry Comission in 1918 when they bought the surrounding land. In 1973 it was sold to a Glasgow school called Crookston Castle Secondary as an outdoor centre. Around the millennium, that school was merged with another, Penilee Secondary, to form Rosshall Academy. At one time it had the reputation for being a 'sick building' so perhaps the staff and pupils appreciated the fresh air of the Shieldgreen Centre all the more!

Right – From Makeness Kip

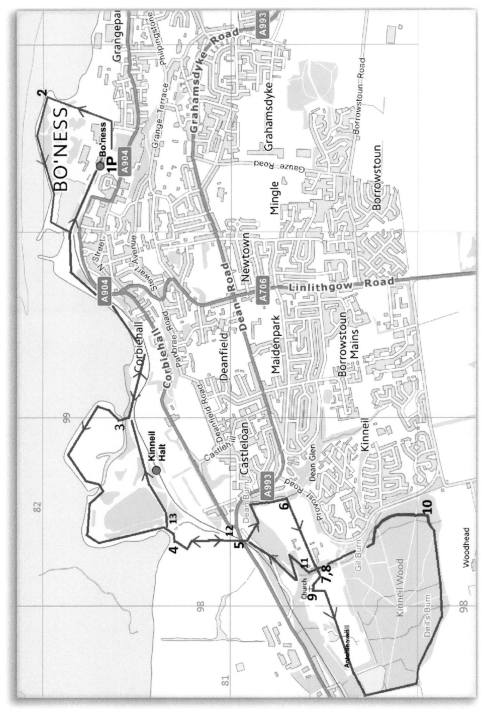

Not to scale

11 • END OF THE ANTONINE WALL
Bo'ness and Kinneil

Sea shore, small nature reserve, stately home with historical church remains and the second last fort on the wall. Very varied underfoot. Check the timetable of the **Bo'ness and Kinneil Railway** on their website. They are very seasonal. Do not attempt this walk on a day when they are running.

The last fort on the wall is in the private Carriden Estate. A 4km walk E along the John Muir Way would bring you to Carriden House. The fort is just inland of it

WE SAW in January: buzzard, little grebe, redshank

MAP OS Explorer **349** Falkirk, Cumbernauld & Livingston.

Distance 13km
Ascent 100m
Walking Time 3h30'
Allow 4h30'
Highest Elevation 85m

PARK Bo'ness station car park, GR NT003 8165

TO GET THERE Take M9 to Jnct 3. Turn R on to A904. Follow brown signs to Bo'ness and Kinneil Railway. Park in station car park, GR NT003 8165, free.

TOILETS None

CAFÉ Bo'ness Bakery, 01506 825 336, North Street, Bo'ness. It is in the Matthew Steele Building. Matthew Steele was a local architect who was active in the Art Deco era. The local Hippodrome is his most famous work. He died in 1937.

THE WALK

1   0.5km; 0m; 8'
Leave the car park in an E direction opposite to your entry. Pass the white picket fence with the green Fire assembly point. Keep the fence on your L. Walk directly across the overflow car park and leave it by a small path still heading E. Pass a building to gain the public road. Turn L, N. At the corner of the road leave it and continue across the green area to the sea. Turn L, W.
GR NT007 817   0.5km; 0m; 8'

2   2.4km; 0m; 36'
Follow the shore line heading generally W. Cross the dam/bridge at the disused dock and continue along the coast with the Kinneil/Bo'ness railway track on your L.

Bugloss

About 1km beyond the bridge you will see the island
which is the Kinneil Nature Reserve on your right with a
boulder causeway leading to it. Cross it if you can. (If it
is impassable follow the water channel for about another
400m to find an easier crossing. Come back to the rough
causeway but on the other side.)
GR NS990 8155   2.9km; 0m; 44'

3   1.6km; 5m; 29'
Turn R, E and then NE to circumnavigate the island.
There should be good birding all along the sea. When
the path turns S find the easy crossing back to the
mainland. Turn R, NW-ish and follow the path round the
headland ending up heading S. When you come to the T
junction at the end of the promontory turn R, SW-ish for
perhaps 50m. Leave the seashore and turn L, S onto a
smaller path into the heathland.
GR NS9837 8127   4.5km; 5m; 1h13'

Camouflaged Turnstones

4   0.35km; 0m; 06'
Almost due S of you is where the railway track tunnels
under the A904. You are going to follow increasingly
small paths as they lead you to the tunnel. On the way
your path goes through a fence. Fork L on to a smaller
path to keep S. You will cross an open sward where a
pipeline is being laid. Keep on your little South-going
path on the other side. By a mature tree look for a stand
of mature birch leftish of you. Head for them on what
pathlets you can find. You should now see the tunnel.
The last few yards are on an even tinier path through
waist high grasses. Cross the fence to gain the rail track.
The little steam train runs here very rarely – high days
and holidays. You can check the website for timetables.
Do not atempt the next leg on days the train is running.
GR NS9835 8095   4.85km; 5m; 1h19'

5   0.7km; 30m; 13'
Walk through the tunnel on the left of the track. At the
other end climb over the fence on your L. You will find a
tarmac roadway and on the other side a grassy area. Go
across both and climb a few metres up through the trees
to find a path heading diagonally up E-ish. Follow it up,
eventually S between a river gorge and some parkland to
the main avenue to Kinneil House. You are on the line of
the Antonine Wall. The avenue follows it.
GR NS986 807   5.55km; 35m; 1h32'

6   0.35km; 0m; 6'
Turn R, W along the avenue or on the grass beside it.

This church served the mediaeval village, which was on the green field to the S. This became an eyesore for the occupants of the big house and was removed and reassembled to form the village of Bo'ness in the mid 17th century.

Roman Fortlet

Enjoy the views of the imposing Renaissance edifice as you approach it. The Museum is in the smaller buildings on the R. It opens at 12.30pm. A notice board close to the main house gives a good description of its architecture and history. Under its impressive walls and to the L find an archway to take you to the wallsteads of the cottage where James Watt developed a, then modern, efficient version of the steam engine – highly secret!
GR NS982 805   5.9km; 35m; 1h38'

7   0.1km; 0m; 3'
Head W across the bridge and immediately take the path on your R. Pause to look at the imposing back of the house.
GR NS 981 805   6.0km; 35m; 1h41'

It was here, in the 17th century, that Lady Alice Lilburn, clad only in a white nightdress, jumped to her death. She had been imprisoned by her jealous husband, a general in the Cromwellian army. She is The Lady in White who is said to haunt the house.

8   0.1km; 0m; 4'
Continue to the remains of the ancient church dating from the 11th century. (see picture on page 61).
GR NS981 806   6.1km; 35m; 1h45'

9   1.3km; 30m; 22'
Go out on to the field to find the line of the Antonine Wall with helpful information boards. Follow the path W through the trees and by the pond to the scanty Roman Fortlet remains. (See picture)
When you have finished exploring the site continue W past a larger pond. Your track soon turns S still beside the water. At the SW corner of the loch take the rough path uphill with fields on your R until, almost at the top, you meet a fence. Turn L, E on the path beside it and follow it along the top of the hill. Ignore paths off to the L. Enter the woodland where the path is less distinct. Cross the stream on a footbridge without handrails – exciting! 50m later turn L on to a mountain bike track.
GR NS9848 799   7.4km 65m; 2h07'

10   1.25km; 25m; 22'
Follow the track as it curves this way and that to join a broad track. Turn L on the broad track and very soon R on to the John Muir Way. Follow it N-ish back to the house.
GR NS982 805   8.65km; 90m; 2h29'

11   0.6km; 0m; 9'
Stay on the path as it passes behind the house and curves R. Soon it becomes a tarmac roadway. You can

avoid the asphalt by staying just above it. Part way down find a path going more steeply down on the right of the roadway. Cross and descend it. Join a wooden walkway constructed across a wet area. This will lead you back to close to the tunnel. Go through.

GR NS9835 8095   9.25km; 90m; 2h38'

12 0.35km; 5m; 5'

Now you will retrace your outward route to the shore by climbing through the fence to the N and taking the little path through the high grasses. Continue to head N on whichever paths are convenient until you reach the sea.

GR NS9837 8127   9.6km; 95m; 2h43'

13 2.4km; 0m; 36'

Turn R, E and follow the asphalt track. You are going to stay between the sea and the railway on whichever tracks keep you heading E-ish. Some 600m, 8', later you should spot the stony causeway you crossed on your outward journey. Ignore it and continue E through the parkland. You will pass to the S of the disused dock to reach a footbridge over the railtrack. Cross and find your car in the car park.

12km; 95m; 3h19'

Right – 11c Church site (Leg 8)

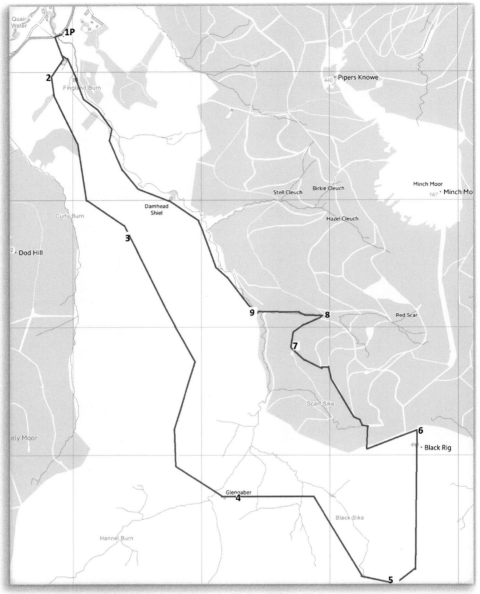

Not to scale

12 • GLENGABER and TRAQUAIR FOREST

A walk on moorland and in forest. Some rough terrain.

Marsh Orchid

WE SAW in June: spotted marsh orchid, bugle, birds foot trefoil, heath bedstraw, bluebells, cuckoo flower, oyster catcher, peregrine plucking place.

MAP OS Explorer **337**, Peebles & Innerleithen

Distance 13.1km
Ascent 460m
Walking Time 4h08'
Allow 5h15'
Highest elevation 463m

PARK just beyond Traquair Village in a lay-by where the road bends to cross the Fingland Burn. GR NT329 3427

TO GET THERE Take the A703 S to Peebles. In Peebles turn L at the roundabout on to the A72 to Innerleithen. In Innerleithen turn R on to the B709 with brown sign posts to Traquair. Pass the junction with the B7062, Cardrona road, in the hamlet of Traquair. Slow down and watch for the lay-by on your L.

TOILETS None.

CAFÉ The Whistle Stop, 12 High St., Innerleithen 01896 830374. If you are a large group, the day before let them know you are coming. They will bake extra scones. To get there return to Innerleithen, turn R on to the A72. The café is about 200m along on the L on the corner of Chapel St. To park you may want to go to the next L turn on to the B709, Leithen Road, and park there. From here you can continue N to Edinburgh after your coffee.

THE WALK

For part of this walk you will be on an arrowed route. Later you will leave it so pay no attention to the waymarkers.

1   0.6km; 30m; 11'
Leave your car and walk across the bridge to find the entrance to Damhead Farm immediately on your L. Walk up the avenue for about 150m and swing R. Go through

the gates to pass behind the outbuildings. (The farmer may ask you to take a different route, depending on what he is doing). Walk up across the field beyond the farmstead. Go through the gate and turn L,S.
GR NT328 3395   0.6km; 30m; 11'

2   1.5km; 115m; 35'
Follow the SW side of the field. Pass to the L, E of a band of trees and an enclosure beyond. Next comes another band of trees, Damhead Wood, which you pass in a similar way. Your track continues to climb S to reach the walls of 2 enclosures. Follow the track between them to emerge on the moorland again.
GR NT3333 326   2.1km; 145m; 46'

3   2.6km; 60m; 50'
Continue SE-ish on the track round the side of Damhead Rig. As your route flattens out pause and look almost due N to try to pick out the white building which is Traquair House. It is this side of a U bend in the Tweed. Continue on the track as it descends and crosses the Fingland Burn. On the other side keep L to pass below the house. Go through a gate into a rough field. Cross the field going just N of E. Go through a gate out on to the moorland.
GR NT3441 3077   4.7km; 205m; 1h36'

4   1.3km; 170m; 37'
Immediately beyond the gate step across a stream as you follow an E going track across the moor. Next cross the more considerable Dean Burn. About 100m beyond the burn take a S, R fork, leaving the established path. Ascend the shoulder between Dean Burn and Black Sike to meet an NE/SW fence on the skyline. Do not go through.
GR NT3545 300   6km; 375m; 2h13'

5   1.2km; 50m; 23'
Turn L, NE with the fence at first. Watch for another fence joining yours from the SE. This is where you leave your handrail and continue just E of N on the crest of the hill to reach the wall at Traquair Forest edge. Do not cross. GR NT355 311   7.2km; 425m; 2h36'

6   1.4km; 0m; 21'
Turn L, SW-ish and follow the wall as it descends ever faster to a gate in the wall. GR NT353 3105. Go through and, ignoring any branches which would lead you upwards, follow the green arrowed path as it zigzags

Traquair is reputed to be the longest inhabited house in Scotland. In the late 11th century and early 12th King Alexander 1st lived here. In 1107 he designated Traquair Forest as a Royal Forest to be preserved as a playground for noblemen. It's now operated by the Forestry Commission and fortunately you don't have to be titled to use it! The present laird of Traquair is Catherine Maxwell Stuart. Her name gives a clue to the various families who have owned the estate. Nowadays they brew several flavoursome beers.

Looking back at Glengabber

down to join a more established track at Glen Cleuch.
GR NT347 318.   8.6km; 425m; 2h57
,

7   1.7km; 35m; 29'
Turn R, N to follow this broad track until it slopes down to
become more metalled at the Camp Shiel Burn. Do not
cross the burn.
GR NT346 330   10.3km; 460m; 3h26'

8   0.6km; 0m; 09'
Turn L, W to descend the muddy burnside path to the
house called Camp Shiel. Go out through their gate and
across the Fingland Burn.
GR NT340 3277   10.9km; 460m; 3h35'

9   2.2km; 0m; 33'
Follow the river downstream passing Damhead Shiel and
Damhead Farm to regain the B709. Turn R across the
bridge to your car.
                                 13.1km; 460m; 4h08'

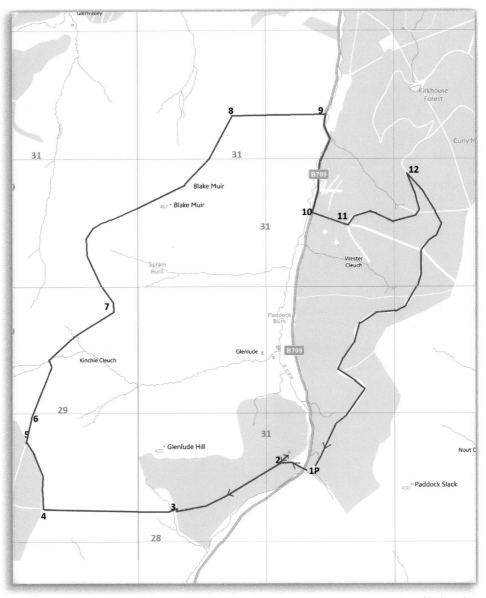

Not to scale

13 • GLENLUDE & SOUTHERN UPLAND WAY (SUW)

Rewilding woodland, open moorland, difficult ascent through harvested forest, some interesting finds and magnificent views. A short cut avoids the difficult bit.

Lapwing

WE SAW in April: lapwing, curlew, skylark, pipit, meadow brown butterfly, hatching frog spawn.

MAP OS Explorer **337,** Peebles & Innerleithen.

Distance 13 km
Ascent 500m
Walking Time 4h30'
Allow 5h30'
Highest elevation 470m

PARK In the parking lot opposite the entrance to Glenlude Forest GR NT313 286. No toilets here.

TO GET THERE Take the A703 south to Peebles. Turn L on to the A72. Drive to Innerleithen. Turn R on to the B709 to Traquair. Stay on the B709 past Traquair and Kirkhouse. Soon a forest appears on your left. The parking lot is at the end of this forest.

CAFÉ The Whistle Stop, 12 High St., Innerleithen. 01896 830374. The day before, if you let them know you are coming with a large group, they will bake extra scones. To get there return to Innerleithen, turn R on to the A72. The café is about 200m along on the L on the corner of Chapel St. Park where you can. You may want to go to the next L turn on to the B709, Leithen Road, and park there. From here you can continue N to Edinburgh after your coffee.

THE WALK

Glenlude Forest is owned and managed by the John Muir Trust – their smallest property – about 1 square mile. This house is for volunteers. In the polytunnel are growing native species which will replace the present forest as it is harvested. This is a step in the rewilding of the reserve.

1   0.5km; 20m; 10'
Cross the A709 and go through the gate on to the access road to Glenlude Forest. Walk to the T junction and turn R. Walk along to the house and polytunnel. Return to the T junction.
GR NT311 286   0.5km; 20m; 10'

2   1.1km; 20m; 20'
Go straight ahead. Follow this wide ride westwards until you come to a sheep fold. Turn R, N up through the trees for a few metres to find a faint path on your L continuing

westwards. Continue to wend your way generally west to reach the edge of the woodland. Follow this edge NW for a few metres to a streamlet.
GR NT3018 2830   1.6km; 40m; 30'

3   1km; 100m; 25'
Descend with the streamlet for a few more metres to the burn below. Cross. Climb up the bank and over or through the fence. From here walk due W across the hillside for about 900m to find another forest.
GR NT 292 283   2.6km; 140m; 55'

4   0.7km; 20m; 13'
Turn R, N and, wiggling to avoid the boggy areas, follow the forest fence to where 2 walls intersect. Climb over the wooden barrier to the forest side. Follow the forest edge N-ish to join the SUW at a stile and gate. Go out on to the moorland.
GR NT291 287   3.3km; 160m; 1h08'

5   0.1km; 10m; 2'
Follow the SUW up Middle Rig for about 100m. Stop at GR NT292 289 and look R, E down the valley to the farmhouse of Glenlude.
                    3.4km; 170m; 1h10'

6   1.19km; 40m; 20'
Continue on the SUW across Yellow Mire Burn, across Kinchie Cleuch Burn and up on to the next top. Go around the shoulder to GR NT297 298. Up above the track on your L look for a square stone sticking up. Go and have a look.
                    4.59km; 210m; 1h30'

There are 13 kists along the full length of the SUW. Each was made by a local artist. This one bears the inscription 'Ultreia' – 'on with your quest'. The 'coins' inside are called 13ths and are there for long distance walkers to take. Each kist has 13 coins with various designs by young artists.

7   2.22km; 50 m; 39'
Continue on the SUW over Blake Muir. As you descend the other side you will see an intersecting fence below you. Spotting this fence is the cue to tell you to leave the SUW. Do not walk to the fence but as soon as you <u>see</u> it turn R, E-ish off the path.
GR NT307 314   6.81km; 260m; 2h09'

8   0.76km; 0m; 25'
As you cross the shoulder of the hillside the valley with

Glenlude Farm was the home of Sheila Bell from 2000 to 2010. She planned to rewild Glenlude but handed the property and task on to the John Muir Trust in 2004. Ugandan born, she trained as a pilot and made her fortune in Africa running her own air transport company and later by running a computer business in the UK.

SUW kist

Cinque Foil, and White Campion

the B709 comes into view. Just below you spot the corner of a wall delineating a field system. Go to this corner and descend with the wall, through a sheep pen and then through a gate to the road.
GR NT3145 3138   7.57km; 260m; 2h34'

9   0.8km; 10m; 13'
Turn R, S and walk along the road, over the bridge across the Paddock Burn and uphill to find a lone tree on the R side of the road. Opposite is where you climb up into the forest to begin the next leg. If you have had enough at this point it is possible to walk on along the road for 2km to find your car.
GR NT3137 3055   8.37km; 270m; 2h47'

10   0.3km; 100m; 25'
Climb the ditch and then use the fence as a rough guide to lead you up the steep hillside. Watch for trip wires hidden in the undergrowth. Part way up take a breather and see the sheep folds below on your R; to the L, cultivation terraces. Reach an intersection with a forestry track. Here you will turn L, N.
GR NT316 304   8.67km; 370m; 3h12'

11   0.94km; 42m; 19'
Follow the broad track as it curves up in a wide S-shaped bend to a T junction with another forestry track. Turn R, S.
GR NT320 308   9.61km; 412m; 3h31'

12   2.99km; 60m; 51'
This track wends through the forest all the way back to your car.
12.6km; 472m; 4h22'

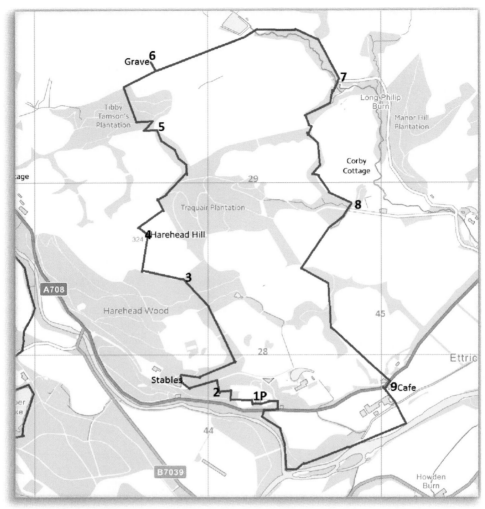

Not to scale

14 • HAREHEAD HILL and TIBBIE TAMSON'S GRAVE

Gardens, two memorials, woodland and open moor all within the Philpshaugh Estate 01750 21766. From this walk there are excellent views of the Duchess' Drive so this is best done after Bowhill. However, avoid the lambing season: March, April and early May. In May and June you may see the salmon leaping at the weir.

The Philiphaugh Estate belongs to Sir Michael Strang Steel. It is operated as a trust with advice from the Duke of Buccleuch who owns Bowhill Estate across the Ettrick.

Covenanters' Memorial

WE SAW in May: garlic mustard, wood sorrel, violets, primroses, wild pansies, forget-me-nots, ramsons. Buzzards, wren, mistle thrush.

MAP OS Explorer **338**, Galashiels, Selkirk and Melrose

Distance 9.2km
Ascent 340m
Walking Time 3h25'
Allow 4h30' plus coffee time.
Highest elevation 324m

PARK At Philipshaugh gardens on the A708, GR NT4425 277.

TO GET THERE, avoiding Selkirk, take the A7 south from Edinburgh. Pass through the small hamlet of Stow and about 5mls further turn right on to B710 signposted Clovenfords. When you reach that village take the A72 exit from the roundabout and IMMEDIATELY turn L on to Caddonfoot Road, the B710 continued. At Caddonfoot turn L on to the A707. Follow it south, across the Tweed and on through the outskirts of Selkirk. Just after the road does a sharp L turn, turn R on to the St Mary's Loch road, the A708. Now you will pass, on the left, The Waterwheel Café (coffee later) and the Salmon Leap Viewing Centre to find, on the right, the entrance to Philipshaugh. Turn in. Ignore R fork. Take the next L possibly signed "Garden". This takes you past the entrance to the walled garden, some cottages and round to beside the polytunnels where you can park. If you are a large party it might be wise to ring ahead, 01750 21766, to make sure they are expecting you.

TOILETS None

CAFÉ The Waterwheel Cafe, 0175022258. GR NT450 277. It is on the A708 beside the Salmon Leap Viewing Centre and just about opposite Philipshaugh Garden entrance. Ring one or two days ahead to tell them when and how many.

They make excellent applecake. It closes at 4pm. However, if you leave Edinburgh at 9am you should reach here around 2.15pm allowing an extra hour for faff time and an hour and a quarter driving time.

THE WALK

0km; 0m; 30'
Find a gardener and enjoy a browse round the poly tunnels. Buy what you want and arrange where to leave it until your return which will be 4pm ish.

0km; 0m; 30'

1   0.3km; 10m; 6'
Leave the garden area in a W-ish direction – not the way you came in. A few metres later turn L at the crossroads. Walk 75m past a clump of rhododendrons on your R. Immediately beyond them turn R into the open woodland. A few metres further brings you to a track. Veer L on to it. The corner of the old tennis court appears on your L. Turn L along its N side to reach the very large Covenanters' Memorial commemorating the Battle of Philipshaugh fought in 1645 when the Covenanters defeated a Royalist force led by the Marquis of Montrose. There are often flowers by its base.
GR NT440 278

The approach to the monument – almost hidden in the trees.

0.3km; 10m; 36'

2   1.2km; 150m; 33'
Beyond the monument go R, N beside the wooden fence, on to the tarmac road and turn L, W. About 100m later take the right fork to pass the stables complex on your L. Zig zag upwards passing behind the buildings. Now the track does a sharp R just below a clothes drying area. Just beyond the clothes lines take a L turn on to a less-used path heading NE-ish through the trees. Pass between old stone ruins and above Philipshaugh House, below you in the trees, overall maintain your NE-ish direction. Walk through the remains of an old quarry which, no doubt, supplied the stone for all the edifices around you. Beyond the quarry look over to your R to see some fields and their boundary wall. You are going to choose the paths which keep you roughly parallel to this wall as you climb. A steep little section brings you level with the top of the fields. Now the track veers slightly L as it continues to climb. The gradient slackens across an intersection of tracks. Maintain your general direction as the route steepens again to reach the open hillside of Harehead Hill.
GR NT435 2843

Yellow Pansy

1.5km; 160m; 1h09'

From Harehead Hill enjoy the views. To the NW across the Yarrow you can see Newark Tower where the Covenanters massacred their captives after the battle. Beyond it is Black Andrew's Wood. On the skyline, almost due W, is Newark Hill with its cairn and to the left of it is Fastheugh Hill and, connecting them all, the Duchess' Drive.

Tibbie Tamson, the spelling of the name varies – Thomson on the stone but Tamson, the vernacular pronunciation, on the notice - lived in Selkirk. She was accused of the theft of a piece of cloth and rather than suffer the consequences she hanged herself. Suicide was not tolerated in the Christian community so she could not be buried within the bounds of Selkirk. However, some felt pity for her and brought her corpse here to a spot in no-man's-land between the boundaries of Selkirk and Philipshaugh. Some reports say she was halfwitted and did not understand the definition of her crime. This may explain the guilt feelings which, to this day, mean that as part of the Common Riding flowers are laid on her grave.

3   0.5km; 80m; 16'

Continue on the track for about 250m and then turn R off it uphill to zigzag NE-ish up to the triangulation point which gradually comes into view. Look for beautiful little purple or yellow wild pansies as you climb.

GR NT4365 287   2km; 240m; 1h25'

4   0.9km; 10m; 14'

When you are ready to move on leave along the wall heading just W of N. Go through the first gateway and cross the next field diagonally to its NE-ish corner by the wood. Go through the gate into the next field. A few metres later find a stile to take you into the wood. Follow the track L for a few metres and then find a small path leading up NE along the wall. Follow this through the woodland first NE and then NW for perhaps 400m. Exit through a gate into a field.

GR NT4369 293   2.9km; 250m; 1h39'

5   0.8km; 30m; 15'

Turn L and pass immediately into another field. Follow the forest edge for about 50m to a gate. Go into the woodland, Tibbie Tamson's Plantation. Go in and follow the track in a generally N direction through and out of the woodland on its N edge. Continue to a fence. Turn R in a NE direction, cross a stile. About 10m later find another stile round the corner of the wall on your L. It drops you right at the grave.

GR NT437 2965   3.7km; 280m; 1h54'

6   1.4km; 0m; 23'

Leave the site by the same stile. Turn L, NE ish to follow the field boundary over the brow of the hill and down to the reservoir at the bottom. Pass by it keeping it on the left hand side, cross the stile and the sleeper bridge to gain the cart track. Turn R downhill. Some 700m later you come to a junction and, if there is enough water, the graceful little waterfall called Corby Linn.

GR NT448 296   5.1km; 280m; 2h17'

7   1km; 20m; 17'

Turn R across the burn and walk up the track a couple of hundred metres to emerge into a field. Immediately turn L, S and climb up to the corner of the field. Go through the gate on your L into the woodland. Ahead of you is a field*. To avoid walking through this field as much as possible you are going to follow the strip of woodland S as far as you can, so turn R through the trees and

then, after a few metres, L. Maintain a S or even E of S direction. Walk down to where a partridge breeding pen bars your way. Go left through the wooden gate into the field*. Continue to follow the field boundary to a gate in the bottom, S, corner. Go through.
GR NT448 289   6.1km; 300m; 2h34'

8   1.5km; 40m; 27'
Follow the track across the crossroads, down through a gate and up the side of the next field heading SW. Go through the gate at the top and turn sharp L through another gate into woodland. Follow the track through the trees ignoring a sharp L turn. Exit at another gate. Turn L, S downhill on the broad track. Follow this track maintaining a southerly direction to the public road, A708. Cross it with care and find the entrance to a little path on the far side.
Turn R on the path to take you to coffee at the Waterwheel Café
GR NT451 278   7.6km; 340m; 3h01'

9   1.6km; 0m; 24'
When you are ready, leave the car park towards the farm buildings and immediately turn L towards the river. Take time to read the information boards and perhaps view the leaping salmon. As you leave the buildings notice the enormous waterwheel on your right. Turn R on the tarmac path as you make your way upstream past the

The fields to the S of the A708 are where the Battle of Philipshaugh was fought on the 13th Sept 1645 as commemorated by the monument visited in Leg 1

Pansy

74

Song Thrush

salmon leap and the Archimedes screw. About 100m beyond the weir take a small path off to the R. Follow this through the woodland until it meets the broad track again. Go straight across to a path which takes you to the confluence of the Yarrow and the Ettrick. Turn R upstream on the Yarrow. You rejoin first the broad track and then the A708 at a point just beyond the entrance to the gardens so turn R, cross the road and a few metres later turn L into the driveway. A few metres later take the little path which climbs up the bank on your left to take you to just beside the walled garden. Turn L and walk round to the cars. Remember to collect your plants if you made a purchase earlier.

Ignoring coffee time the statistics are:

9.2km; 340m; 3h25'

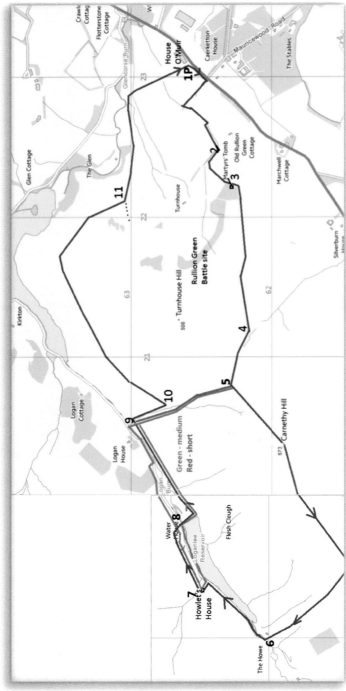

Not to scale

15 • HISTORY in the PENTLANDS

The wild mountain feel close to the city and full of history, some gruesomely recent. Three options are given so you can match the walk to your available time or energy.

MAP OS Explorer **344**, Pentlands, Penicuik and West Linton

Short option
Distance: 7.5km;
Ascent: 325m;
Time: 3h20'
Medium option
Distance: 8.5km;
Ascent: 375m;
Time: 3h45'
Long option
Distance: 11.5km;
Ascent: 525m;
Time: 5h
Highest elevation 573m

PARK in an old road fragment at House O' Muir on A702. Go beyond the houses and park in the dead end.

TO GET THERE Take A702 S. Pass Flotterstone. Up the hill and immediately round the bend from Flotterstone take the first R. The entrance is marked House O'Muir but there is no roadside signpost.

TOILETS None

CAFÉ Secret Herb Garden, 07525 069 773, on Old Pentland Road GR NT 2605 665. The kitchens close at 4pm but the greenhouses stay open. You need to get your order in before 4pm. To get there drive N on A702. Just beyond Easter Howgate turn R indicated Roslin. After about half a mile turn L through Easter Bush. Reach a roundabout. Go straight across. At traffic lights turn L on to the A703. Watch for Damhead sign. Slow down and watch for a bus stop and immediately take a small unclassified road going off on the R beside a walks sign. Go to the T junction with Old Pentland Road. The entrance to the Secret Herb Garden is opposite. On leaving it is best to go L to the traffic lights on A701. Turn L and later L again on to the by-pass. This route avoids the dangerous junction at Hillend.

Or you could use Cobbs at Craigddon, 44 Biggar Road, open

9am to 6pm. Tel. 07930 564574. This is a family business which started in Drumnadrochit. Telephone in advance if you are a large group.

THE WALK

1   0.9km; 55m; 20'
Walk SW along the pavement to the first field entrance. Leave the pavement and climb over into the rough area of trees. Stumble through the trees, NW-ish, to a stream. Now follow the stream SW-ish keeping out of the fields as much as possible. Where the stream turns abruptly right, leave it and go through the gate on to a track.
GR NT225 6235   0.9km; 55m; 20'

2   0.4km; 45m; 11'
You are going to follow the edge of this field which, in the 19th century, was the site of one of the biggest sheep markets in Scotland. Many drove roads must have led here. First turn R and follow the track to the sheepfold. Leave the track passing the sheepfold with it on your R. Ascend SW-ish to the trees. By continuing a few metres further find the Martyrs' Monument set into the edge of the forest and surrounded by railings.
GR NT2222 623   1.3km; 100m; 31'

Rullion Green memorial

The monument commemorates 2 victims of the Battle of Rullion Green where an exhausted band of Covenanters from Galloway and Ayrshire were routed by Royalist troops led by Thomas Dalyell on 28th November 1666. They were 900, a ragged band with few cavalry. The Royalist were 3000 strong and with the back-up of 600 cavalry. Few Covenanters escaped, dying either on this field or being executed. One wounded soul did manage to limp off in the direction of his homeland only to perish in the hills. He probably used the Roman road as a guide for the first part of his way. Later the cairns near Mendick Hill (Walk 19) would have been land marks for him. His grave is on the shoulder of Black Law near Dunsyre in sight of his home hills. The leader of the cavalry, Major Joseph Learmont, is buried in the graveyard of Blackmount Parish Church at Dolphinton. (See Walk 25)

3   0.6km; 74m; 17'
Leave the monument by following the tree edge S-ish to a gate and a broad track ascending W-ish beside the trees into the next field. The fence on the left hand side, W of this field gives the direction of travel. Stay more or less parallel to it as you cross into the next field and ascend the little hill to the remains of a prehistoric fort. GR NT2165 622. It probably looked to the Covenanters much as it does today! From here look ahead along the same fence line, past the fence at the end of your field,

to find a wall heading NW up into the hills. This is your next directional handrail. Go there and find the path beside the wall.
GR NT211 6217   1.9km; 174m; 48'

4   1km; 60m; 21'
Follow the path up to the col between Turnhouse and Carnethy. Turn L and go over the fence. Here you have options.
GR NT2079 6228   2.9km; 234m; 1h09'

Short and Medium Options
0.8km; 0m; 9'
Turn R, N again. Descend, very steeply in places, from the col, to the bridge across the Logan Burn.
GR NT2045 630.   3.7km; 234m; 1h18'

Short option Do not cross. Go to Leg 9

Medium Option continued
1.3km; 35m; 20'
Cross the bridge to the road. Turn L, SW. Pass, on your R, the entrance to a house. Continue some 250m on the road beside the field wall to where it turns up away from the road. Clamber up the bank and follow the small track SW-ish under the overhanging boughs of the trees and parallel to the road below. Follow this sheep track as it curves round the steep side of Gask Hill above Loganlea Reservoir. After some 300m you reach a small stream feeding the loch. On the opposite bank is Howlett's House ruin. Scramble down and across to it. GR NT1935 6245. When you leave follow the instructions in Option B of Leg 7.
                                              5km; 269m; 1h38'

5   Long Option
2.5km; 148m; 53'
From the col turn L, S and climb Carnethy. Follow the path down to the col between Carnethy and Scald Law. Here turn R, WNW-ish, to descend to the Howe valley.
GR NT189 6195   5.4km; 382m; 2h02'

6   0.6km; 10m; 10'
Turn R, NE-ish to reach Loganlea Reservoir. Follow the metalled road to just before the fisherman's harbour. Here turn up off the road to the remains of Howlet's House.
GR NT1935 6245.   6km; 392m; 2h12'

7   This leg can be done in 2 ways:
A   0.6km; 25m; 12'
Leave the upper side of the ruin to the NW. Look down

Howlett's House. Hidden in the grass around the ruined house are the remains of quite an extensive site. There are various theories about the nature of this place. One idea is that there may have been a place of worship here with supporting buildings which might have predated St Catherine's Kirk, now drowned in the waters of Glencorse Reservoir. Another idea is that it was a fortified home. In the days of the Covenanters this silent place would have been a thriving community.

at the burn below. The stream as it descends to the loch makes a sharp right bend. A few metres before this bend look for a path up the steep bank opposite which joins another sheep path contouring round Gask Hill above the reservoir. Having picked out the way scramble down to the burn and up the other side on your chosen route. Follow the paths to the bottom end of the loch and scramble down to the dam.
GR NT198 626   6.6km; 417m; 2h24'

B 0.6km; 0m; 9'
If you do not fancy this narrow track through the heather you could walk along the road to the dam. GR NT198 626 This option takes 25m off the total ascent.
                                         Med: 5.6km; 269m; 1h47'

8   0.9km; 10m; 15'
Cross the dam. Clamber over the fence and turn L to follow the Logan Burn downstream using any convenient tracks until you reach a bridge across the burn, some 800m. Do not cross it. Above on the road is Logan House.
GR NT205 630.
Medium option   6.5km; 279m; 2h02'
Long option   7.5km; 427m; 2h37'

In January 1985 this place was the site of gruesome murders. Corporal Andrew Walker waylaid 3 fellow soldiers after they had withdrawn the wages for Glencorse Barracks from a bank in Penicuik. Walker was armed with a gun which he had signed out in his own name from his own armoury. He shot one soldier at the beginning of the robbery, another during the journey and the third, who was forced to drive the vehicle, here. He had to abandon the vehicle because there was a locked gate across the road in those days. The vehicle and the victims were quickly discovered but Walker himself was hunted for 3 days through the hills before being caught. The money is hidden somewhere in the heather and is still undiscovered. Walker was given a 27 year sentence, served in Saughton. He had a stroke in 2009 and was released one month early in Dec 2011.

9   0.3km; 70m; 12'
Go through the gate ahead and turn R up the valley. Some 200m up the valley spot a small tree on the other side of the burn. This is a marker for you to look for a track, somewhere on your L and above you roughly on contour 300, going off through the heather in a N-ish direction.
GR NT2065 6285
Short option   4km; 304m; 1h30'
Medium option   6.8km; 349m; 2h14'
Long option   7.8km; 497m; 3h

Old Pentland Cemetery

Glencorse Reservoir was constructed around 1822. Under its N corner lies the ruins of St Catherine's in the Hopes Kirk. In severe drought the waters recede to expose its remaining stones. One story suggests a chapel may have been built here by Henry Sinclair a henchman of Robert the Bruce in the 14th century. St Catherine was She of the Wheel fame. The legend says she was to be executed on the fiery wheel but at her saintly approach the wheel shattered. The sword which beheaded her was less vulnerable! Anyhow the firework now bears her name.

10 1.9km; 0m; 29'

Follow your chosen track to contour round Turnhouse going first NE-ish for about 1.1km above Glencorse Reservoir. Chose the easiest routes through the rough terrain but stay approximately on the 300 contour. Still contouring gradually swing E for some 300m and then SE-ish for perhaps another 500m to join the main track from Turnhouse to Flotterstone.
GR NT222 631.

Short option	5.9km; 304m; 1h59'
Medium option	8.7km; 349m; 2h43'
Long option	9.7km; 497m; 3h29'

11 1.4km; 15m; 23'

Turn L, E and descend to cross the first burn. Immediately across it turn R, S-ish. Ascend through the trees and follow the track down to House O'Muir and your car.

Short option	7.3km; 319m; 2h22'
Medium option	9.1km; 364m; 3h06'
Long option	11.1km; 512m; 3h52'

Old Pentland Cemetery

When you finish your coffee leave your car and walk up the road to the L to the Old Pentland Cemetery. As you go in notice the Watch House to guard against body snatchers. 60 dead Covenanters from Rullion Green were buried here. The old church founded by Malcolm II served the area before Rosslyn Chapel existed. It was Malcolm's daughter Cora who may have given her name to the Falls at New Lanark (Walk 5)

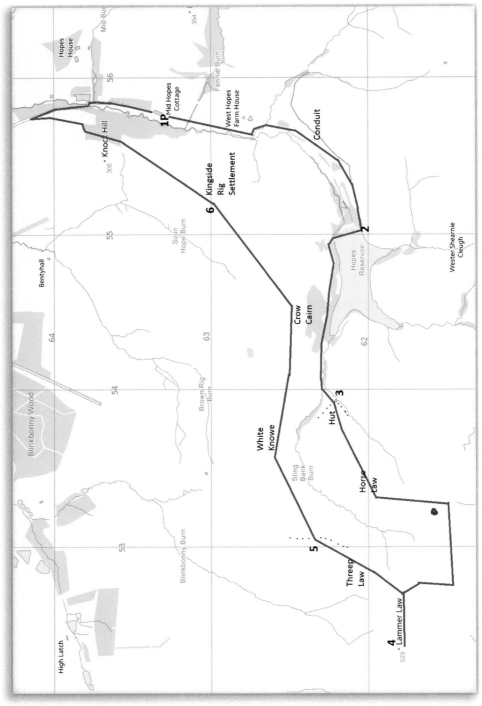

Not to scale

16 • LAMMER LAW and HOPES RESERVOIR

A walk with lochside, moorland and a prehistoric ring. Rough going in places and some steep slopes. Wonderful views on a clear day.

WE SAW in December: a raven and a kestrel engaged in aerial combat. The raven was croaking loudly. It was a stand-off. A mountain hare in blue and white; 2 flocks of linnets; lots of mallard; a sunlit Isle of May looking very close.
In addition in April: willow warbler and heard a cuckoo. Primroses.

MAP OS Explorer **345** Lammermuir Hills – East sheet

Distance 11.4km
Ascent 415m
Walking time 3h32'
Allow 4h 30'
Highest elevation 527m

PARK in the car park between East Hopes and West Hopes, GR NT558633.

TO GET THERE Go east on Edinburgh Bypass. Take A68 Dalkeith bypass. Just over 3 miles later turn left on to A6093 signposted Pencaitland. Drive right through Pencaitland and turn right on to B6355 towards Gifford. From the crossroads* just SW of Gifford take the unclassified road to Longyester. At Longyester farm turn left NE. Half a kilometre later turn right to The Hopes. 2.5 km later, after crossing the Hopes Water and driving past East Hopes farm buildings, park in the designated area.

Black headed gull

CAFÉ in Gifford. Lanterne Rouge Café, 1 Main St. EH41 4QH. 07961 965240. If you are a big group, alert them the day before. To get there return to the crossroads* mentioned above. Turn R into the village. The café is on the R near the church.

THE WALK

1   1.9km; 60m; 33'
Walk south from the car for about 600m. Do not go over the stile which is straight ahead but follow the track left. Go through the gate over the cattle grid. Once across the little stream take the right, lower fork. You are still heading south but you are above the Hopes Water. Continue uphill for about 650m. Here you will find a water

conduit crossing the track. Turn right along its narrow way to reach the dam of the reservoir. Enjoy the junipers growing around – quite rare now.

GR NT550 620   1.9km; 60m; 33'

2   1.3km; 35m; 22'

Walk across the dam. Notice the inscription in the wall at the far side telling you that these stones came from the old Calton Jail – restraining water now rather than people!

Calton Jail was on the site of St Andrew's House on Regent Road just below Calton Hill. In 1817 it was built in grand Greek classical style belying the horrendous conditions within. After executions in public stopped they continued within the jail with the bodies being buried under what is now the car park. Richard III was not the only one! Their skeletons still remain.
The jail was demolished in 1930. One inmate who later became Secretary of State used stones from the jail for his garden path – walking triumphantly through history.
More of the stones were used to make this dam.

Ascend steeply north up the bank opposite, just to the left of a willow. Cross the stile at the top. Continue to ascend for a few metres and then swing left, westish, to follow a narrow path parallel to the reservoir and just above the bank of deciduous trees. Follow this path along the loch. At the far end go through the gate and straight ahead, gradually descending to Sting Bank Burn below. About 300m from the gate look across SW-ish to spot a shed in the valley between Bleak Law and Horse Law. Cross the burn to the hut.

GR NT539 622   3.2km; 95m; 55'

3   3km; 242m; 1h10'

From this hut 3 paths diverge. One goes up the valley of the Sting Bank Burn; one goes up the valley between Bleak Law and Horse Law and the middle one, yours, ascends Horse Law on an initial bearing of 257°. Follow this up. About 500m beyond the top of the steep climb and out SW-ish across the moorland watch for a little lochan down on your right. About 50m after the lochan you will find a path going R in a W-ish direction. GR NT533 6145. Take it. About 600m later at a grouse butt your track intersects a path heading almost due N. Turn R on to this northerly track. (OS maps show a fence accompanying this track. It no longer exists but has been replaced by a new one some 50m west.) Follow this north-going track to where 2 fences meet in a point. Take the track running beside the most westerly fence gently ascending. This fence is your guard rail for the next little

N	Berwick Law
19°	Isle of May
70°	Monynut Edge Wind Farm
250°	Moorfoot Hills
W	Pentland Hills
300°	Ochil Hills
325°	Lomond Hills

The Cairn

The Dam

section. Pass through a gate in the new fence mentioned above. Now watch for a gate* in your guide fence and, directly opposite, the broad, boggy track going west to the Lammer Law cairn. If the weather is not too extreme you may be able to find enough shelter round the large cairn to eat lunch. If not wait till later in the descent.
GR NT5235 618   6.2km; 337m; 2h05'

4   1.1km; 0m; 17'

Return east to the gate* in the fence but this time go through and take the path heading just north of east across Threep Law. Ignore the first paths going off to the left but at about 250m from the gate take the fork to the left on a bearing of 62°. This track becomes more distinct as it gradually swings round to be heading just east of north. You should come to a much broader track just where a fence joins it from the right GR NT531 624. This fence will be your guard rail for the next 4km of the walk. Turn off the broad track to follow the fence NE-ish.

7.3km; 337m; 2h22'

5   2.5km; 78m; 46'

First descend to a col and then begin to ascend White Knowe. About 300m after the col you will see a gate coming up. Before you reach the gate and just before the electric fence starts, cross the guard rail fence. Follow the broad track on the other side E-ish over White Knowe, through a gate, over Crow Cairn and along the ridge, now heading NE-ish. Where the path forks take the upper, left leg to stick with the fence. Just after you begin the descent you will find the prehistoric settlement of Kingside Rig to the right of the path. Take a moment to explore it and enjoy the views.
GR NT552 629   9.8km; 415m; 3h08'

6   1.6km; 0m; 24'

Continue to follow the fence to a wood and a crow trap. Go through the crow trap area and enter the forest on a path. Follow it through the trees and out into a newly planted area. Go across this to the fence beyond. Turn downhill with the fence to a gate which gives you access to the fields beyond. Follow the fence on your right hand side down through these fields to the roadside. Go along the roadside fence till you find the gate to the road. Turn R on it and walk back to your car.

11.4km; 415m; 3h32'

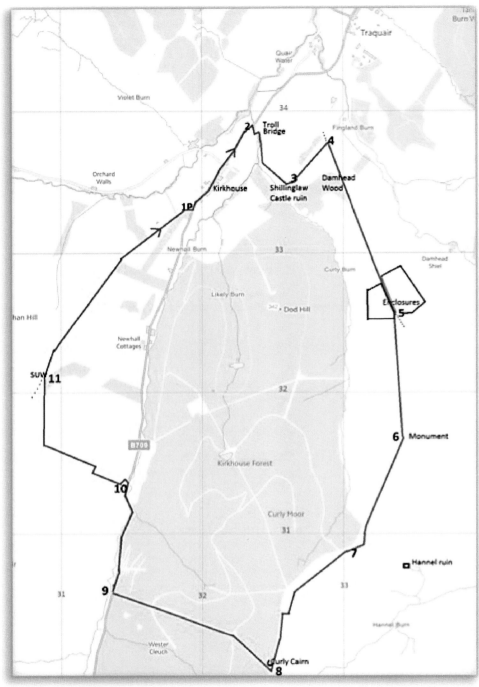

Not to scale

17 • LEARMONT DRYSDALE MEMORIAL

A walk through forest and across moorland visiting the memorial to a Scottish composer. Beautiful views. Room for ingenuity in finding best routes through a few patches of rough, boggy terrain.

MAP OS Explorer **337**, Peebles & Innerleithen

Distance 10.8km
Ascent 510m
Walking Time 3h35'
Allow 4h30'
Highest elevation 412m

PARK Parking lot just past Traquair Church GR NT320 334. There has been a church in Kirkhouse since 1116 dedicated to St Bride. The present building was erected in 1778 on the ruins of the old one.

TO GET THERE Take the A703 S to Peebles. At the roundabout turn L on the A72 to Innerleithen. From there turn R, S on the B709. Go straight through Traquair and follow the sign to Traquair Church, 1 mile further in Kirkhouse. Immediately past the church, in the middle of a beech hedge, find the somewhat concealed entrance to the Parking lot.

TOILETS None

CAFÉ The Whistle Stop, 12 High St., Innerleithen. 01896 830374. The day before, if you let them know you are coming with a large group, they will bake extra scones. To get there return to Innerleithen, turn R on to the A72. The café is about 200m along on the L on the corner of Chapel St. Park where you can. You may want to go to the next L turn on to the B709, Leithen Road, and park there. From here you can continue N to Edinburgh after your coffee.

THE WALK

1   0.6km; 0m; 9'
Turn L, NE back on the B709. After about 600m, 9', you come to Kirk Bridge. Do not cross.
GR NT327 339   0.6km; 0m; 9'

2   0.6km; 50m; 14'
Go through the hedge on your R and step over the wooden fence. Follow the Curly Burn upstream for a short distance to a troll bridge. Trip, trap across. Continue upstream on the other side. Where a metal gate leads

into a field do not go through but step over the wooden fence to its R (closer to the burn) and continue upstream. Stick to the wall on your L rather than to the burn itself. Ascend with the wall to a gate in a transverse wall. This is the site of the old Shillinglaw Castle erected by the Murray family.

GR NT326 334   1.2km; 50m; 23'

3   0.4km; 20m; 8'

Go through. Turn slightly L, NE-ish and ascend between the stony outcrop and the spring for a few metres. Find a faint track heading NE parallel to the wall on your L and a few metres above it. Cross this field with this track to a gate. Go through.

GR NT329 3367   1.6km; 70m; 31'

4   1.2km; 100m; 28'

Turn R, SE-ish uphill with the well-defined track. Follow it up past Damhead wood and out across the moorland. After about 1 km you have a wall on your L. Continue through the 2 gates to exit these enclosures. Where you leave the enclosures leave the track and turn R, S.

GR NT337 326   2.8km; 170m; 59'

5   1km; 120m; 27'

The wall on your R, S gives the line of ascent for Damhead Rig. Climb up. Once past a small cairn, veer R and finally, on the summit, reach the Learmont Memorial Cairn.

GR NT334 316   3.8km; 290m; 1h26'

Learmont Drysdale, 1866-1909, was an Edinburgh composer. Rejected by Edinburgh Music School for his lack of orchestral skills he got a job as an organist in London and one year later was admitted to The Royal Academy where he won the top award for composition. In 1904 he came North again, to Glasgow where he worked for a year before returning to Edinburgh and his beloved mother. She died in May 1909 of pneumonia which killed her son only one month later aged 42. His memorial was erected in 1937. His elder sister Janey lived nearby and was able to attend the ceremony. She continued to live in this remote spot until her house burned down in 1949. She died shortly afterwards aged 87.

6   0.8km; 10m; 13'

Continue S across the broad summit gradually veering slightly R, W. Follow any convenient paths through the heather to lead you down towards the corner of the forest. Two gates take you past a new planted enclosure and on to the SW-ish ascending hillside with the forest on your R.

GR NT332 310   4.6km; 300m; 1h39'

Bog Cotton

7 1.3km; 70m; 27'

This area can be soggy so keep looking ahead and choosing the driest route. Half way up pause for a rest and look back into the valley. Down below you will see the wallsteads of Janey Drysdale's home called the Hannel. Across the valley is the house called Glengaber (Walk 12). After about 600m, 16', ignore the first firebreaks, one with a fence, going off more or less from the same point. As you reach the top of the climb look for a wooden slatted bit in the barbed wire fence on your right. Climb over and continue along the forest edge to reach Curly Cairn, a low crescent of stones which marks a firebreak and a fence heading NW-ish.

GR NT325 3002   5.9km; 370m; 2h06'

8 1.3km; 0m; 20'

Follow this firebreak with its fence as it descends, gradually at first and then steeply to the B709. Do not be lured aside by any crossing tracks. Pick your steps carefully and use any convenient pathlets - you do not need to stick slavishly to the fence. In the logged area beware of trip wires - the remains of old fences.

GR NT3138 3058   7.2km; 370m; 2h26'

9 0.8km; 10m; 13'

Once on the tarmac turn R, N and walk about 800m crossing the Paddock Burn, passing a lay-by and just round a L curve finding a way up the steep grassy slope to a gate above.

GR NT3141 3137   8.0km; 380m; 2h39'

10 1.1km; 130m; 30'

Go through the gate and ascend with the wall on your R. Go through a sheepfold using the gates and continue to follow the wall up. Almost at the top of the hill turn R with the wall. Go through a gate and continue across the pasture in a N direction to join the Southern Upland Way, SUW, at the corner of the wood.

GR NT309 321   9.1km; 510m; 3h09'

11 1.7km; 0m; 26'.

Follow the SUW as it wiggles N and NE down to the B709 in Kirkhouse. Turn L to find your car.

10.8km; 510m; 3h35'

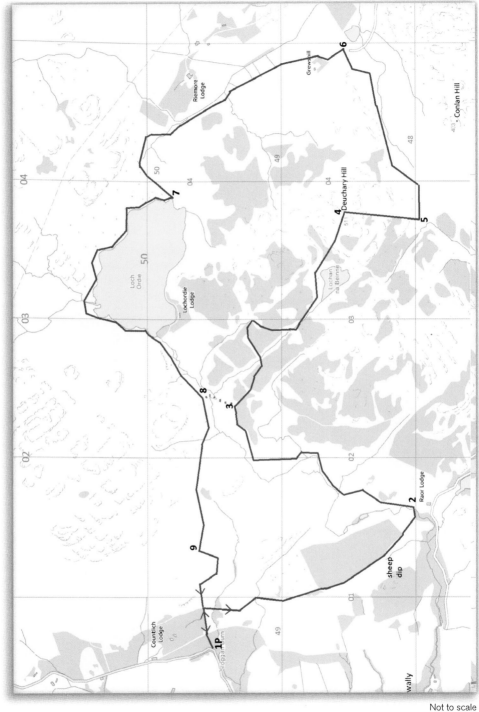

Not to scale

18 • LOCH ORDIE and DEUCHARY HILL

An open hill walk with 360° views. One very steep section both up and down but not vertiginous.

Eyebright

WE SAW in June: buzzard, stone chat, wren, skylark, curlew, meadow pipit, mistle thrush, robin, heath bedstraw, butterwort, red rattle, bell heather, chickweed wintergreen, forget-me-not, foxglove.

MAP OS Explorers **379** Dunkeld, Aberfeldy & Glen Almond and **387** Glen Shee and Braemar. The walk spans both.

Distance 14.75km
Ascent 480m
Walking Time 4h35'
Allow 5h35'
Highest elevation 511m

PARK 1km up Guay road at a sharp L bend. Parking space directly ahead. Do not park on the road. Do not block other cars. GR NO 0062 495

TO GET THERE take the A9 N past Dunkeld. Immediately past Dowally Craft Centre turn R on the unclassified road signposted Guay. Pass some houses and drive on up through the trees to the sharp L bend.

TOILETS Convenience woods.

CAFÉ The Foyer Café, Birnam Arts and Conference Centre, Station Rd, Dunkeld, Perthshire PH8 0DS. Phone: 01350 727674 To get there take the Dunkeld exit from the A9 S. Immediately turn R towards Birnam on the Perth Road. Pass the Birnam Hotel and immediately turn R into Station Rd. The Arts and Conference Centre with its café is on the R. It closes at 16:30. Park where you can. Alternatively use Taste of Perthshire, Bankfoot which is open until 7pm. Phone: 01738 787 696. About 5mls S of Dunkeld take the Bankfoot exit from the A9 S.

THE WALK

1   **2.2km; 90m; 42'**
    Walk up the E-going path through the trees. Go through a gate and continue about 150m to a crossroads* with

another track. (You will come back down here at the end of the walk). Turn R, S along it. After about a km you have a wood on your L and opposite, a sheep-dipping station. Beyond the wood your track curves L, through a gate with a waterfall below and then crosses the Dowally Burn to a T junction. Turn L, NE-ish.
GR NO 0161 4801   2.2km; 90m; 42'

2   1.9km; 70m; 36'
Walk with this track up the valley of the Dowally Burn. After about 30' start to look for a bridge ahead crossing the burn. When you see it stop and look for a gate in the fence on your R. It is about 150m before the bridge. Turn R, SE-ish through the gate.
GR NO 0235 494   4.1km; 160m; 1h18'

3   2.1km; 250m; 57'
This woodland ride wiggles its way up for about 1.5km to reach Lochan Na Beinne. Now you are following a thin path continuing to climb E past the loch and up to the trig point on Deuchary Hill. Enjoy the superb views. Even on a windy day you can usually find a neuk round the craggy summit to have a breather.
GR NO 0374 4851   6.2km; 410m; 2h15'

4   0.65km; 0m; 30' (extra time to allow for the angle of descent)
Leave with care on the abrupt path heading roughly S through the rocky terrain. Where a choice exists use the more worn route. Continue to follow this pathlet steeply down to a T junction of paths some 500m down. Turn L, E.
GR NO 037 4795   6.85km; 410m; 2h45'

5   1.4km; 10m; 22'
About 1.3km later keep R, NE-ish at a fork. Continue to the tarmac road by Children's Loch and turn L, NW-ish.
GR NO 049 4857   8.25km; 420m; 3h07'

6   2km; 30m; 18'
Pass the entrance to the house called Grewshill. Some 12' later leave the tarmac as it turns R, across the Buckney Burn, into Riemore Lodge. You continue NW-ish, off the tarmac now, beside the burn. Eventually cross the stream and come to a T junction. Turn L. Follow the track down to Loch Ordie and its lochside path. Turn R, N on the shore.
GR NO 0388 4982   10.25km; 450m; 3h25'

Use your compass to identify:
N	*Cairngorms*
280°	*Schiehallion*
	(pointed mountain)
260°	*Ben Lawers group*
235°	*Ben Chonzie*
160°	*Perth*
030°	*Lochnagar*
025°	*Glas Maol and the*
	Glenshee Mountains

Riemore Lodge is now available as a holiday cottage. It is part of the 4000 acre Riemore Estate operated as a shooting business.

Forget-me-not

7 2.4km; 20m; 38'
Follow the loch round its N and W sides down to the
SW corner where you meet the Dowally Burn again as
it leaves the loch. Keep R and continue SW-ish with
the burn to a junction in the tracks. At this point you
may recognise the bridge below you as the same one
you used as a marker on the way up. It serves the same
purpose now. You veer R, W. You will not cross the
bridge.
GR NO 0245 4958   12.65km; 470m; 4h03'

8 1.2km; 10m; 19'
Walk in a generally W-ish direction for about 1km. Now
the track descends and swings round R and flattens out.
On the L is a little ridge culminating in a rocky outcrop.
Just before this outcrop find a grassy track to the L, SW.
Take it.
GR NO 0129 496   13.85km; 480m; 4h22'

9 0.9km; 0m; 13'
Follow this track as it curves down to pass the
crossroads* of Leg 1 and to take you back to your car.
                                   14.75km; 480m; 4h35'

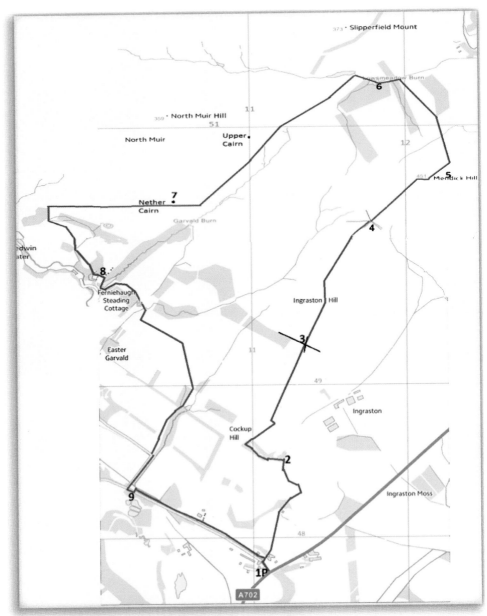

Not to scale

94

19 • MENDICK HILL

A beautiful walk through farmland and open hills. 360° views from the top and flowering rhododendrons and irises by the lochan in early summer.

Bog Asphodel

WE SAW in late April buzzards, sparrowhawk, pied wagtail, greywagtail, mallard, pheasant. Primroses, anemones. In late June or July the rhododendrons and irises should be in bloom.

MAP OS Explorer **344** Pentland Hills Penicuik & West Linton

Distance 11.5km
Ascent 350m
Walking Time 3h30'
Allow 4h30'
Highest elevation 451m

PARK Immediately you turn off the A702 on to the Dunsyre/Garvald road there is a green space on your left with ample room for parking.

TO GET THERE Take A702 south from Edinburgh for about 26 miles. Just beyond sign for Dolphinton turn R on to unclassified road signed Garvald, Dunsyre.

TOILETS None

CAFÉ Cobbs at the Craigdon Centre at the Lothianburn roundabout on the A720, City Bypass. Warn them ahead of time if you are a large group. Tel. 07930 564574.

THE WALK

1 **0.6km; 40m; 13'**
Walk westwards along Dunsyre Road for about 100 metres. Where the houses end on the R, N side of the road look for a track. Follow it between the house and a strip of woodland. You will return through this woodland at the end of the walk. Go through a gate into fields and turn R, E then N. The track goes uphill past more woodland and through another gate. Continue past some sand quarries to reach the strip of woodland on the east side of Cockup Hill.
GR NT109 479   0.6km; 40m; 13'

2 **1km; 65m; 21'**
You need to get to the ridge which runs NE-ish from Cockup Hill. Go through a gate into the woodland and

straight uphill to the top of the trees. Turn R along the top fence and climb a rickety gate to enter a field. Continue along the top boundary of the field to find a gate in the hollow. Go L through the gate into the rough ground of Cockup Hill. Follow this rough ground in a NE-ish direction through a broken field boundary to a complete field boundary.
GR NT1138 4925.   1.6km; 105m; 34'

3   1km; 35m; 19'
The fence running just E of N ahead of you will be your guide along Ingraston Hill. Cross the junction on to the R, S side of the guide fence. Follow it up then through a gate taking you to the N side of the fence. About 950m, 13', where 3 fences meet, go through a gate in a soggy corner to reach the slopes of Mendick Hill.
GR NT117 5015   2.6km; 140m; 53'

4   0.8km; 141m; 27'
Climb, still maintaining your bearing of approximately 40°, up the subsidiary ridge of the hill. At the top of the ridge turn E to cross the col and ascend steeply to reach the summit of Mendick Hill. Enjoy the views. To the N you can see West Water reservoir. The summit of Dundreich is visible on the eastern skyline.
GR NT121 506   3.4km; 281m; 1h20'

5   1.2km; 0m; 25'
You need to descend to a point nearly due N but it is easiest to leave the top along its NE ridge and gradually swing round picking your way down the steep slopes to head for the angled strip of woodland which is due N of you GR NT122 511. Cross the awkward fence into the open land between the strips of forest. Cross the open land diagonally to reach the Lowsmeadow Burn at the corner of the woodland on your left. Turn upstream between the woodland and the water to enter an open area beside some ponds. These would have been the fish ponds for the Slipperfield estate. Cross to the north side of the ponds and enjoy the rhododendrons and the irises if they are in bloom – late June or July. The ponds are fed by 2 burns – the Lowsmeadow Burn which you walked along and the Dry Burn.
GR NT117 514   4.6km; 281m; 1h45'

6   1.9km; 20m; 14'
Leave the area by the track beside the inaptly named Dry Burn going NW-ish. Turn L on a broad track heading SW-ish across the moorland. About 200m later keep to the

Bronze age grave or kist

West Water reservoir was completed in the 1960s. What had been a small knoll became an island washed and eroded by the waters. In 1992 at a period of drought the water keeper noticed unusual stone structures appearing on the island. This with the find of some shards of pottery made him call the archaeologists. Seven early Bronze Age kists were found as well as evidence of other burials. In the least disturbed of the kists a skeleton was wearing a necklace of lead beads – the earliest evidence of the use of metallic lead in Scotland. The kists have been moved and can be seen just off the Slipperfield Farm road and south of West Linton golf course, GR NT139 5185.

The cairns, of which there are three along this route, are thought to have been waymarkers for the early people. Each traveller would have placed another stone on the pile. This tradition is carried on by Monro baggers who are expected to add a stone to the cairn on top - this more as a mark of triumph than as a guiding post. The first cairn on your present route has been extensively robbed for neighbouring walls. The second one, Upper Cairn, is much larger and the third, Nether Cairn, is the best preserved of this type of cairn in Scotland. It is possible that the wounded Covenanter escaping from the massacre at Rullion Green on 28November 1666 may have limped past these markers to find his rest and demise at Blackhill Farm about 2km to the NW of Nether Cairn. (Walk 25)

Coot

right. Go through a gate and about another 200m later you may just be able to discern a lump on the hillside which is the remains of a once large cairn. About another 400m later you should get a good view of Upper Cairn. Continue on the good track for approximately another 700m, 10', until you see the great Nether Cairn on your right. Leave the big track and cross the moorland to visit the cairn and maybe even climb to the top. From up there you may be able to spot Upper Cairn which you passed earlier.

GR NT105 504   6.5km; 301m; 1.59'

7   1.8km; 10m; 37'

After your visit continue to wend your way westwards for a further 800m across the moorland using any convenient paths to reach a well-defined path running N/S. Turn L, S, on it. Pass between Locket Gate Wood and Fold Wood, through 2 gates and across the top end of the farmyard of Medwynbank to reach a track, in fact the one you were on before your visit to Nether Cairn. Turn R on it.

GR NT1005 497   8.3km; 311m; 2h36'

The farmhouse is a listed building as is a sawmill within its precincts. One occupant, John Hay Forbes, was created Lord Medwyn at the turn of the 19th century.

8   2km; 40m; 34'

Descend for about 50m and turn L, SE-ish. Pass just to the south of a little loch. Follow this track first uphill and then round and down to pass close by a house on your right. Just beyond it keep right and ascend again round the shoulder of a little hill and across a field. Go through the gate and cross the next field diagonally to your right, SE-ish, to enter some woodland and find a broad track. Follow this as it winds down through the woods and across some fields beside the trees. It finally descends to the public road at a gate. Continue downhill on the road for 200m to the T, crossing the old railway line just before the junction. You will access this old track for your return journey.

GR NT102 486   10.3km; 351m; 3h10'

9   1km; 0m; 15'

At the T junction turn L and immediately start to look for ways to scramble down to the old railway track below on your left. Be careful because soon after you join it there are some holes in the middle of the track. Follow along it to a fence. Cross it, a road and another fence to continue your journey on the disused railway. At the end step over a fence to find your outward route. Turn R and then L along the road to the vehicles.

11.3km; 351m; 3h25'

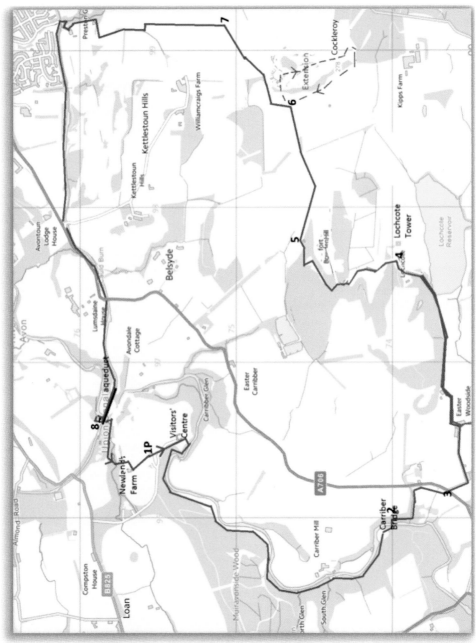

Not to scale

20 • MUIRAVONSIDE and BEYOND

Rare breeds, riverside, hill, cross country, canal and a spectacular aqueduct. Suitable for inclement weather **but not after heavy rain**. An extension takes you to the prehistoric fort on Cockleroy Hill.

WE SAW in May: wood sorrel, primrose, violet, bluebell, comfrey, wood anemone, lesser celandine, Solomon's seal, leopard's bane, garlic mustard, cowslip, wild cherry, lesser stitchwort, greater stitchwort, chickweed, penny cress, ramsons, white day nettle, red campion, germander speedwell, forget-me-not, cuckoo flower. Buzzard, jay, green woodpecker, wren.

Muiravonside Estate was owned by the Stirling family who sold it to the local authority in 1978. A member of that family was instrumental in setting up the SAS.

MAP OS Explorer **349** Falkirk, Cumbernauld and Livingston

Distance 12.6km
Ascent 290m
Walking Time 4h
Allow 5h
Highest elevation 278m

The extension over Cockleroy Hill brings it to Distance 15km; Ascent 400m; Walking Time 4h30'; Allow 5h30'

PARK In Muiravonside car park. GR NT963 755

TO GET THERE Take exit 4 off M9 then second exit off the roundabout on to A801 indicating Bathgate. At next roundabout take first exit indicating Linlithgow. About 1 mile later on the right find the entrance to Muiravonside Country Park.

CAFÉ at the Visitors' Centre employs special needs staff. Call John on 01506671290 to tell him how many walkers and when. He will stay open later than the stated 3pm if there is a biggish group AND he will bake extra scones.

TOILETS At the Visitors' Centre and Newlands Farm.

THE WALK

1 **2.9km; 90m; 53'**
From the car park the Visitors' Centre is in a S direction. It is signposted. The toilets are there so, if you are a group, people can wander down, use the facilities and congregate there for the start of the walk. The River Avon walkway is just to the south of the Centre. Follow signs to it and turn R, upstream. Follow the walkway uphill and

Water Avens

down stairs but always staying more or less parallel to the river. After about 1.8km cross N Glen stream on stepping stones with the help of an interesting chain support. 300m later you cross S Glen stream in the same way. Some 700m later cross the river by Carriber Bridge, a stress-laminated wood bridge – the first of its kind in the country!
GR NT959 740   2.9km; 90m; 53'

2   0.7km; 65m; 18'
Turn R still upstream. Cross the next little bridge over a tributary and immediately turn L to ascend the edge of the gorge of the little stream in an easterly direction. Go carefully. At the top of the gorge go into the field on the right, S. Follow the fence which divides you from the road to a gate about 200m along.
GR NT9615 736   3.6km; 155m; 1h11'

3   1.8km; 50m; 32'
Go through the gate and cross the busy road. Take the minor road opposite. Follow it for about 450m passing Wester Woodside and then Easter Woodside where you leave the tarmac and take the broad track on your left towards Lochcote House. Follow this driveway past some houses and through a kissing gate beside the locked entrance gates. Ascend past the main house on your left to leave the grounds by an unlocked gate. Go straight ahead into a green area with sparse trees. Notice Lochcote Tower ahead of you on the right.
GR NT975 739   5.4km; 205m; 1h43'

4   0.9km; 40m; 18'
You leave the area by the track heading N beside the rhododendrons. Veer leftish through the wood and into the field on the north side – opposite side to the reservoir. Follow the track across the field in a N-ish direction to contour round to a gate which gives access to the woods above – not to the field. Ascend this track and circumnavigate Bowden Hill. Later zigzag down roughly N to an E/W track. Turn R, E.
GR NT977 746   6.3km; 245m; 2h01'

5   0.7km; 20m; 12'
Follow this track over the rise for about 500m, 7' or 8', to reach a gate. GR NT984 746. Do not follow the track as it turns right and descends. Instead go straight ahead following the wall to reach a ruined cottage.
    * EXTENSION: If you are feeling energetic you can pop up Cockleroy Hill from this point. As you

Lochcote Castle was a 17th century building which occupied the whole of this green area. The stub of building remaining is from an angle tower of the original castle with a more recent addition on top to make it a doocot. At some point the castle burned down and was replaced by an enormous Lochcote House on the same site. Around 1850 there are records of plans by a Mrs Derby to take down parts of the house and by the end of the 19th century it had been completely replaced by a stable block. There is a remnant of this at the N side of the site. Half buried in the grass there are many large blocks of stone from the demolition. There is no evidence of when the present house was built but it seems likely that Mrs Derby built herself the present more manageable house on the elevated site with a view. Where you are standing, she had her huge stable block for horses and carriages.

Wild Geranium

The aqueduct was built around 1820 by Baird with advice from Telford. It has a metal skeleton clad in stone thus allowing it to be slimmer than an all stone structure. The whole thing is hollow and an access door allows engineers to go inside for inspection and repair. It is the longest and tallest aqueduct in Scotland.

Meadow flowers

approach the hill scan the steep hillside for the access route. It will be curving upwards on your left hand side. Ascend the hill and go along its crest to descend the other side by the tourist route. At the bottom turn sharp right between the hill and the forest wall. Walk down to a gate. Go through and follow the field boundary on your right back to your starting point. This adds 2.2km; 82m; 42'; to your statistics from now on*.

GR NT984 746   7km; 265m; 2h13'

6   1km; 15m; 27'
Continue to follow the line of the field edge as it turns left and descends steeply through whin to a track which takes you to a gate on the E side of the field tucked under the tail of Cockleroy Hill. Go through or over the gate and follow a little path across 2 more fields to reach an untidy junction of fields with a line of trees stretching away to the N.

GR NT991 751   8km; 280m; 2h40'

7   4km; 10m; 1h01'
Cross the wall junction and follow the woodland strip for about 450m. There in a kink in the wall you will find a stile taking you on to a farm track. Turn R, N. Follow the track as it wends its way down past the golf course and finally to the Union Canal. Take the towpath in a westerly direction. About 2.5km later enjoy the 810ft walk across the aqueduct.

GR NT966 759   12km; 290m; 3h41'

8   0.6km; 35m; 19'
At the end of the aqueduct turn R down the stairway which leads under the canal and down to the Avon. Take the R spur on the stairway at the bottom. Turn R upstream beside the tributary called Bowhouse Burn. Follow the track up, across a bridge, almost to the top of the hill. Find a 3-way junction. Take the leftmost way down to the Bowhouse Burn and cross it on a wooden bridge. Take the steeply ascending path up the steps to Newlands Farm, a good venue for children. There are toilets here. Continue through the farm to the car park.

                    12.6km; 325m; 4h05'

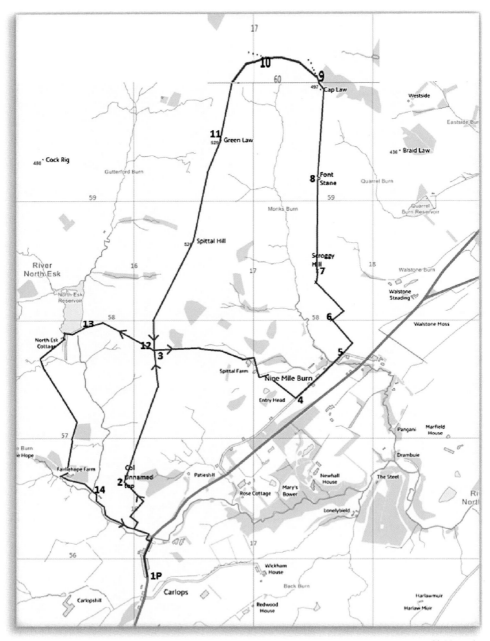

Not to scale

21 • NINE MILE BURN TO CARLOPS – two ways

A broad ridge walk with long views on a clear day. There are 2 variations on this walk. Option 2, the shorter, uses the bus or cars to make it circular. The full walk is a figure of eight, on foot all the way. It is best tackled when the days are long.

Unripe Puffball

Nine Mile Burn is actually 11miles from Edinburgh but the old Scottish mile was longer – hence the Nine.

Carlops, Karlynlippis (1315), means Witches' Leaps. Of an evening witches were supposed to jump from the big rock above the car park to a sister rock now gone.

WE SAW doing Option 2 in a very mild November: 2 voles, 2 buzzards (one being hassled by a crow), 2 kestrels (one at the beginning of the walk and one at the end), 1 raven croaking loudly so the other one was around somewhere, a flock of fieldfares, 8 whooper swans on the reservoir. Loads of puffballs by the burn and 2 buttercups!

MAP OS Explorer **344** Pentland Hills, Penicuik & West Linton.

Option1
Distance 13.6km
Ascent 660m
Walking time 4h41'
Allow 5h45'
Highest elevation 530m

Option 2 Bus to Nine Mile Burn and walk back
Distance 9.5km
Ascent 440m
Walking time 3h17'
Allow excluding bus 4h20'. The longer time is to allow for some difficult terrain along the river particularly tricky in wet weather.

PARK in the designated car park in Carlops GR NT161 559. For Option 2 cross the road and catch the Stagecoach Bus 101 which at time of writing passes at 9.20am. Get off at Nile Mile Burn and walk up the side road to the R angle bend. Read on from Leg 5.

TO GET THERE drive S on the A702 to Carlops.

TOILETS none.

CAFÉ Cobb's Café in the Craigdon Centre at Lothianburn roundabout on the A720, the Edinburgh bypass. Tel. 07930 564574.

THE WALK

1   **1km; 100m; 25'**
     Leave the car park in Carlops and walk north through

the village on the right hand side of the road. As you leave the village look for the '30' painted on the road. Cross carefully. Take the track heading north westish and signposted Buteland. Go to the bridge below Patie's Mill. Cross Carlops Bridge and go through a kissing gate beside a beech hedge. Follow the path and hedge through another gate. Turn right and climb up a few steps to a fence. Do not go through the gate. Instead turn L and ascend with the fence to a right angle bend. Continue to follow the fence path for another 100m. Turn L uphill and ascend steeply to the top of the un-named hill.
GR NT159 5659   1km; 100m; 25'

Patie's Mill was a cotton mill owned by the laird of Newhall estate. It is now a private home.

2   1.2km 110m; 29'
Go N across its broad summit and then down into a col, not following the path which cattle may have turned into a quagmire. Best to stay east of the path and find the driest way down and across the col to find an E/W path. Follow it W-ish for a few metres to a small outcrop of rock. Climb up round this rock to regain the faint NNE path, just as it ascends out of the col quagmire, on its way up Patie's Hill. On the long shoulder you pass through a flattish area before the path steepens again to pass a small windmill and satellite dish and finally reaches the top of the hill. Continue to follow the path as it veers round to just west of north and descends to a fence with a gate leading on to a broad east/west track.
GR NT1619 5775   2.2km; 210m; 54'

Patie's Hill is a reference to the pastoral comedy, 'The Gentle Shepherd' by Allan Ramsay, a local writer of the 18th century.

3   1.5km; 0m; 23'
Turn right, east, on this track and follow it downhill past Spittal Farm and to the quiet public road beyond. Turn left, NE.
GR NT171 574   3.7km; 210m; 1h17'

The word 'Spittal' indicates a hospital of sorts may have been here in earlier times.

4   0.4km; 10m; 7'
Walk along the road crossing a bridge and passing some houses to a sharp right angle bend. Do not go round the bend but instead pass through the kissing gate opposite.
GR NT1759 580   4.1km; 220m; 1h24'

5   0.6km; 50m; 14'
Follow the signposted walk around 2 sides of this field and climb the stile to exit into a whinny area. Turn right, NE, by the fence.
GR NT1759 580   4.7km; 270m; 1h38'

6   0.4km; 40m; 10'
Follow the fence to the corner. Turn L, NW still beside

Ringlet

a fence. 250m later find a stile over the fence leading you just east of north and on to Scroggy Hill. About 100m further up cross another stile to take you on to the hillside proper.
GR NT1748 5831   5.1km; 310m; 1h48

7   0.75km; 115m; 23'
Follow the path up Monk's Rig almost due N to the Covenanters' Font Stane on Cap Law
GR NT1751 592   5.85km; 425m; 2h11'

The monks were on a route which took them from Dunfermline to the abbey at Newhall. The Font Stane is of mysterious origin. It may have been a wayside stop for the monks traversing the Monk's Rig or it may have been used by the Covenanters. John Cochrane in "Pentland Walks" published in 1908 refers to it as the "base of an ancient cross". But where could the cross have gone? Does it lie buried in the peat?

8   0.8km; 35m; 16'
Continue to ascend with the path. It passes to the NE of the summit of Cap Law and flattens out. When the path veers slightly right and begins to descend DO NOT GO WITH IT. Instead go straight ahead remaining at the same height.
GR NT175 6005   6.65km; 460m; 2h27'

9   0.55km; 10m; 9'
Now you begin to walk a broad arc around the top of the valley formed by the Monks Burn and its tributaries. The grassy path becomes a bigger track used by loggers. As this track begins to descend, at a shallow cutting, leave it on a faint path to your L.
GR NT1672 5951   7.2km; 470m; 2h36'

10 0.6km; 50m; 14'
The path swings round to be heading almost due south. Follow it, deviating occasionally to avoid treacherous boggy areas in the col. Ascend Green Law.
GR NT1672 5951   7.8km; 520m; 2h50'

11 2km; 35m; 34'
Descend Green Law and meet a fence. Follow the fence south over Spittal Hill. Continue to follow the FENCE when it leaves the path and drops down to meet a broad track heading east/west.
GR NT1619 5775   9.8km; 555m; 3h24'

12. 0.7km; 0m; 12'
Turn R in a westerly direction towards the North Esk Reservoir. Follow this track west for about 300m. At this

point when you are due east of the reservoir dam take a left fork off the main track and follow it down to the reservoir passing a hut on the way. It is sometimes easier to walk on the grassy verge. Choose the easiest way
GR NT1556 5795   10.5km; 555m; 3h36'

There were seven long graves found on the island in the reservoir. They probably were from the early Christian period.

13. 2.1km; 75m; 40'

Cross the dam and continue on the track as it zig zags past North Esk Cottage signposted Carlops. Just over a kilometre later descend past Fairlihope Farm. Just before the road crosses Fairliehope Burn turn left through a small gate to enter an area of new planting just above the stream. Follow the path through the trees and through a gate into a field. Walk diagonally down across this field to cross a stile and a metal bridge without guard rails to reach the east bank of the North Esk River. Here it is no more than a mountain burn.
GR NT1555 5652   12.6km; 630m; 4h16'

14. 1km; 30m; 25'

Turn right, off the track, to follow the burn. There are some difficult stretches on this narrow path as it negotiates the steep banks of the burn. Go carefully. After about 700m you will reach a kissing gate. Pass through and follow the path and beech hedge to come out at a bridge. Upstream is the waterfall which powered Patie's Mill.

Continue to the main road. Cross and turn right through the village to the Car Park.
13.6km; 660m; 4h41'

Harebell

Great Crested Grebe

22 • PORTMORE SNOWDROPS

A walk through woods, around a loch, through a prehistoric settlement and over moorland above a stream.

Snowdrops

Bracket fungus on oak

WE SAW in March:

Leg 1   two buzzards circling above us as we left the cars, snowdrops, aconites and crocuses in the woods.
Leg 2   tufted duck on the loch, lichen on the loch wall.
Leg 3   jays in the trees.
Leg 4   roe deer in the woodland.
Leg 5   a heron on the lochan by the farm,
Leg 6   a kestrel in the valley of the Longcote Burn.

MAP OS Explorer **337** Peebles and Innerleithen and OS Explorer **344** Pentland Hills. The walk spans both maps.

Distance 12.9km
Ascent 205m
Walking Time 3h36'
Allow 4h30'
Highest elevation 360m

PARK on the roadway outside the Scots Pine café just north of Eddleston, NT243481.

TO GET THERE Take the Peebles road, A703, south from Edinburgh. Eddleston is 4mls north of Peebles and 20mls south of Edinburgh.

CAFÉ Let the Scots Pine Café know the day before that you are coming and how many in the party. They close at 15:30. Tel No. 01721 730365.

TOILETS There are toilets in the Scots Pine Café but they don't open till 10:30. However the first part of the walk takes you into woodland with lots of 'convenience' trees.

THE WALK

Buzzards, snowdrops, aconites and crocuses.

1   **2km; 65m; 40'**
Head north along the remnants of the old road which runs parallel to the A703. 500m later you enter the woodland and emerge close to a lodge-house and avenue. Cross the avenue and go round behind the house very close to their back garden fence, where you will find a narrow way between the fence and the stream

107

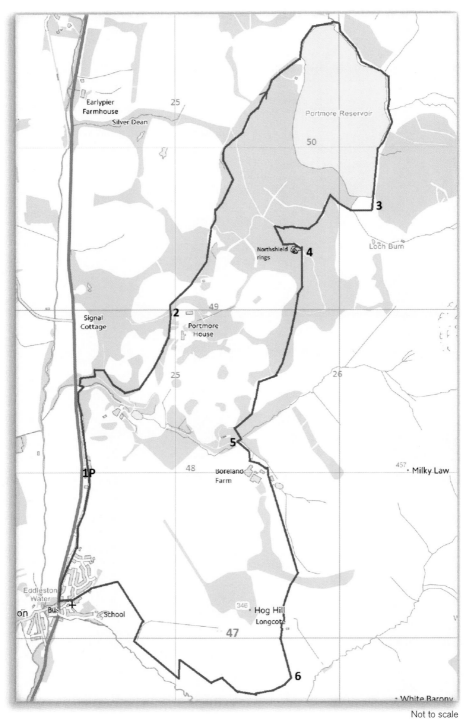

Not to scale

Portmore estate was created in 1732 when the second Earl of Portmore, who also owned the Aberlady estate, bought the land from the Black Barony. The village of Northshields then occupied the site of the present house and gardens. The village was cleared.

The family title died out when the fourth Earl died in 1835, childless. The McKenzie family had acquired the property in 1798. Sir Walter Scott was a regular visitor during the life of Colin McKenzie. A descendant, Walter Forbes McKenzie, was the MP responsible for the 1852 Act of Parliament which, for over a century, banned pubs from opening on Sundays. It was during his time that the present house was built. It was designed by David Bryce in 1850 and is Grade A listed. It is now owned by Londoners, David and Chrissie Reid, who helicopter up for weekends and holidays. Chrissie is responsible for the restoration of the walled garden. The gardens are open on certain days in summer and during the Scotland's Garden Scheme. Private visits can be arranged.

Portmore Loch

which leads to a bridge. Cross. Snowdrops are all around you. Avoid walking on them where you can. Go towards the fence opposite the bridge and find a track. Turn right on it and go for about 100m. Look back at the fence. It has turned away in a northerly direction. Leave the track and walk parallel to the fence beside the snowdrops. After about 75m you will be almost beside the fence. Turn R, E-ish, uphill till you find a broad woodland ride. This now-quiet way leads from the old quarry to Portmore House. Probably back in the 18th century it was a noisy, muddy way as the stone was transported for the building. How times change! Turn right, SE-ish, on it and follow it up as it contours round the hill. Enjoy the panorama of snowdrops below. Follow the path to enter a field through a wooden gate. Cross the field diagonally still following the track. It turns up N along the woodland and takes you through a gate to the back avenue of Portmore House. The house is just below you. Turn left and follow the avenue. Soon on the right you will see the spectacular walled gardens below you. (See page 111)
GR NT251 491   2km; 65m; 40'

2   2.7km; 30m; 43' Tufted duck, lichen.
Follow the broad, upper track. The kennels are below you. Ignoring all exits to your right and a couple of field entrances further up on the left, finally reach Portmore Loch which, before it became a reservoir, used to have eels, much enjoyed by the local community. It is fun to walk up beside the dam wall for a good view across the loch and its birds. The wall has a beautiful pattern of lichens on it. Circumnavigate the loch.
GR NT262 4965   4.7km; 95m; 1h23'

3   1.2km; 50m; 23' Jays
Where the track, now heading S, leaves the southern shore of the loch by some reed beds go through the gate and turn right, just S of W, across the neighbouring field. Ford the stream at the far side. Climb up the next field still following the fence to a gate in the top corner. Go through. Cross the broken down stone wall. Turn right and follow an indistinct path as it swings round to the left and becomes a track which meanders uphill, just S of W, through the heather.
On your way up, pause to enjoy the views across the loch to the Pentlands beyond.
500m later join a broader track. Turn left, SE-ish. Follow this track as it curves up and round to the Northshield Rings which you will find close to the path on the right. Find the broad entrance way and go in to explore the Rings.
GR NT2575 4935   5.9km; 145m; 1h46'

*There is evidence of human habitation in this area from 10,000BC.
This settlement started with 2 defensive rings with 7 large circular huts
inside measuring between 6 and 9m across. Each would have housed
many people. Around the time of the Roman invasion of Britain a
third defensive ring was started perhaps in response to the news of the
Roman approach. The Roman advance north was rapid and there was
not time to finish the outer ring. It is incomplete on the W side.
This whole area was well populated in prehistoric days. The Milkieston
Rings, behind and above Eddleston, are the remains of a very large
settlement used right up to mediaeval times. Many of the hills around,
like Cavarra, have smaller settlements on them. You will get distant
views of them during Leg 6.*

4   1.6km; 0m; 24' Roe deer.
Leave the Rings by continuing on the same track by
which you arrived, heading S. Ignore a path to the left
which heads E. Continue south for almost 1km where,
on the left, a gate and a quad bike crossing take you into
a field. Follow the fence to the right, round and down to
a gate in the lowest corner of the field ignoring both the
first gate and an enclosed area. Go through the lower
gate into the woodland and follow the track contouring
through the trees. About 100m later take a small path
descending steeply to the broad track below.
GR NT254 4819   7.5km; 145m; 2h10'

5   1.7km; 50m; 30' Heron
Cross the bridge and ascend on the broad track to
Boreland Farm. As you reach the farm take the left fork
and then the second turn on your right. Now you are
heading, just E of S, out of the yard past a large animal
shed on your left and through a gate. Check the lochan
on your left for a possible heron or other birds. Continue
to ascend on the broad track. Pass through a strip of
woodland. About 100m beyond the trees, where the
main path swings left, turn right off it and cross the open
land passing by a telephone pole. You are above and just
W of the dwelling of Longcote. Find a broken down wall.
Cross it and follow it S for perhaps 50m to a gate. Pass
through and continue along the track for approximately
250m to pass through another gate on to open moorland
on the south side of Hog Hill.
GR NT2571 4673   9.2km; 195m; 2h40'

6   3.7km; 10m; 56' Kestrel
Follow the track as it contours round W-ish. As you walk,
look across the valley of the Longcote Burn to the skyline
above. There on a hilltop you may be able to make out
the irregular walls of the mediaeval settlement associated
with the Milkieston Rings. Straight ahead, westish,

Walled garden

The first mention of a church on this site was in the notes of the Bishopric of Glasgow in the 12th century. The present church was built in 1837 but it still retains the Flemish bell which is marked 1507.
The accommodation block of the Inn was the old school which took boarders from all over Scotland and beyond. Although condemned in 1883 it remained the village school until 1993 when the new school, which you saw earlier, was built. Children first?

across the main road, the white house with a tower is The Black Barony Hotel in the centre of the estate from which Portmore was carved. About 50m before you reach a fence you will find a left fork which takes you diagonally down to a gate. Go through and remaining at that level go forward for about 150m to find a path on your left angled back and down towards the stream below. Descend. Once down turn right to follow the path through a gate into a field. The new school is in front of you but you are going to follow the boundary on your right round the field to its top, N, corner where a gate takes you on to a path descending left, through another gate, to the village. Stop by the church. Below you are the sleeping quarters of the Horseshoe Inn.
Continue to the main A703 at the side of the Horseshoe Inn whose accommodation block is mentioned above. Turn right, N, to follow the way of the old road back to the cars.

12.9km; 205m; 3h36'

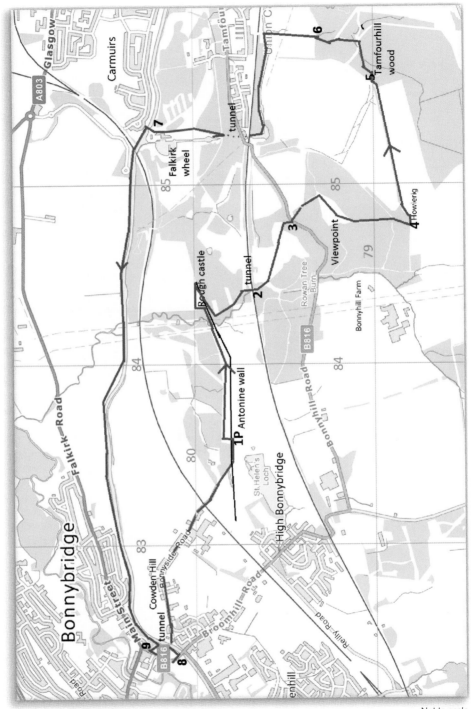

Not to scale

23 • ROUGH CASTLE and the FALKIRK WHEEL

History and engineering. A good walk for wet weather, lunch in the café a possibility.

The Wheel

There used to be 11 locks connecting the Union Canal to the Forth Clyde Canal. Using them took a full day. The Falkirk Boat Lift replaces 9 of the locks and takes about half an hour. The original plans replaced all 11 but cut through the Antonine Wall. It was decided to save the Wall at the expense of some inconvenience for boat users. The Wheel is the only rotating boat lift in the world. Since the boat 'baths' are counterbalanced it uses little power – enough to boil 5 domestic kettles - making it environmentally friendly and economic. The designer used his 8 year old daughter's Lego to model the system!

Archimedes

Antonine Wall

WE SAW in January: buzzard, herons, goosander, tufted duck, little grebe and possibly kingfisher.

MAP OS Explorer **349**, Falkirk, Cumbernauld & Livingston

Distance 10.9km
Ascent 105m
Walking Time 2.58'
Allow 4h
Highest elevation 120m

PARK Near Bonnybridge by the Antonine Wall, GR NT835 798.

TO GET THERE Take the M9 N. You will see the great metal statues of the Kelpies beside the M9. Follow signs for the Falkirk Wheel. When you leave the M876 still following the Falkirk Wheel signs you turn sharp right and go through a roundabout. About 1 mile later you reach another roundabout. Here stop following the Falkirk Wheel signs. Instead turn R on to the A803 to Bonnybridge. At the next roundabout, in the village, go straight ahead on to the B816 to cross the Forth Clyde Canal. Take second L on Foundry Road following brown Antonine Wall signs. Follow the road round a U bend and climb up past several new houses. You will walk this section at the end of the walk so note some reassuring landmarks for yourself. Near the top of the hill the road veers left and narrows before crossing the Glasgow/Edinburgh railway line on a bridge. Next pass some trees and Bonnyside House on your left. Beyond the trees and just after a left bend in the road where the dirt track begins you should be able to park on the verge.

TOILETS None

CAFÉ at the Falkirk Wheel.

THE WALK

1   1.5km; 0m; 22'
Leave the track and enter the open land to the N by the pedestrian gate. This is the area of the Antonine Wall. To the S you can see the Carlisle/Perth railway track. Later you will go under it. Now walk E along the high parapet of the Antonine Wall to the S of the ditch. This is where

the Roman soldiers might have patrolled.

Ignore a hard surfaced road which accompanies you on the right for a short way. Pause before your high parapet descends steeply. Look ahead, E, to get a fine view of the 3 lines of defensive fortifications of Roughcastle fort. Now go carefully down the steep slope, cross the Rowantree Burn on a foot bridge. Further upstream this burn came through a tunnel below the Carlisle/Perth railtrack. You will use the tunnel later. For now, once across the burn and the soggy area beyond, climb up the steep side of the Fort. Further along go out of the N gate of the Fort and veer L to see the stake defence pits. Cross back S and go E to find more boards marking parts of the Fort. From the last of these, The Annexe, head S-ish to reach the outermost, furthest S, rampart. Turn W to follow it back towards the Rowantree Burn. Just before the stream a staggered gate leads you off S on a marked walkway. Through the woods you come to a cross roads. Turn R to reach the tunnel under the railway. Go through.

GR NS844 7966   1.5km; 0m; 22'

(The times given are for straight walking. You may need to add sightseeing time.)

Around AD142 the Romans, under the command of Antonius Pius, built this secure belt along Scotland's waistline The wall stretches from the Clyde to the Forth. It was the northern border of the Empire but was manned for only 20 years. Constructed with an earthen wall on a rubble base it has eroded much more than Hadrian's Wall. Roughcastle was the second smallest fort on the wall but is the best preserved.

Defensive post holes

2 0.9km; 40m; 18'

Once through the tunnel you cross the burn and soon find a small path heading R, S. Follow this to join a broad track heading in the same direction. At a wide crossroads keep up L and follow the track as it ascends and snakes first E then NE and finally S to reach the B816.

GR NS848 7945   2.4km; 40m; 40'

3 0.8km; 10m; 13'

Cross carefully and take the broad track opposite ascending SE to a T junction. Turn R towards the Viewpoint. When you reach it pause to enjoy the panorama.

Continue in the same direction. At a junction keep L, S and soon begin to descend to yet another T junction. Turn R and 100m later meet an E/W path at a crossroads.

GR NS8478 788   3.2km; 50m; 53'

The Tunnel

4 0.8km; 15m; 14'

Turn L, E, and follow this path as it zigzags and ascends through fields to reach Tamfourhill Woodland at a gate. Go through and keep L.

GR NS8551 7898   4.0km; 65m; 1h07'

5 0.5km; 20m; 12'

Follow this track for a couple of hundred metres to where

This is an area of Community Woodland on the site of an opencast coal mine which closed in 1996. The trees were planted in mitigation by Coal Contractors.

The Canal Tunnel

Before the bridge was built, Bonnybridge was called Bonny Water being on the banks of that stream. More recently it is famous for the 300+ UFO sightings from its streets. Their frequency is supposed to be related to the story that the true Stone of Scone is buried near here. Apparently the Stone attracts aliens!

it turns sharp R, E. Leave it here and continue in your N-ish direction on a little path past the seat and by the fence. Follow this up and down as it weaves it way to the edge of the woodland and joins a broad track heading N.
GR NS858 793   4.5km; 85m; 1h19'

6   1.5km; 0m; 23'
Follow the track N to the Union Canal. Cross and turn L, W on the towpath. Soon you reach 2 locks and the turning basin. Pause. Go through the tunnel ahead of you beside the canal. As you walk, above your head is the Antonine Wall, the Carlisle/Perth railway and the B816. Below your feet are several old mines. Fortunately both the ceiling and the floor are heavily reinforced. When you emerge from the tunnel go forward to the beginning of the aerial waterway to get wonderful views. North, across the Carse of Stirling, are the Ochil Hills with their high point – Ben Cleuch. To the NW is Ben Vorlich and Stuc a Croin. Beyond them are the Grampians. To the E is Grangemouth with its oil refinery and to the left of it on a clear day you may be able to pick out the Kelpies. Having enjoyed the panorama retrace your steps to where you can go left and down to the Visitor Centre. On the way down you can see the interlocking cog wheels which raise and lower the barges in their 'baths'.
GR NS853 801   6.0km; 85m; 1h42'

7   When you leave the centre go down to cross the Forth Clyde Canal. Turn L, W. Follow the towpath to Bonnybridge.

8   Go on to the B816. Turn R. Do not cross the bridge. The road curves R. There is a garage on the right with a large parking area.
This garage was once the corn mill for the area. There are mentions of it as far back as 1506.

9   Walk down across the parking area in front of the garage keeping to the R. Go through the Radical Pend, the tunnel under the canal.

This is the oldest surviving tunnel in Scotland. It dates from 1786. In 1820 it became known as the Radical Pend when weavers, who were rising against poor working conditions, were collecting near the Antonine Wall. The radicals were betrayed to the militia by a fellow weaver. The heavily armed government force surprised the unsuspecting workers by advancing on them through the Pend. The broken, defeated weavers were dragged pack through the pend to be incarcerated in Stirling Prison.

On the other side you ascend to join the road you drove up on your arrival. Spot your reassuring landmarks as you walk to your car.
(4.9km; 20m; 1h16') [10.9km; 105m; 2h58']

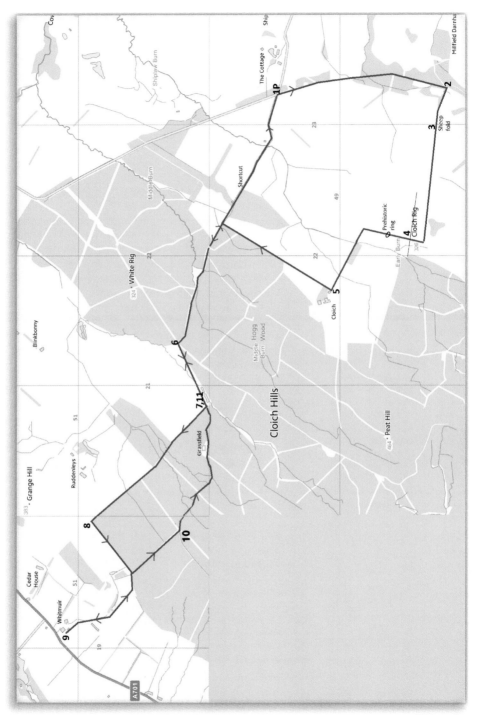

Not to scale

24 • SHIPLAW to WHITMUIR RETURN

A lunch-under-cover walk. Some very rough terrain. Good for cold or wet winter days. Deep snow makes it very difficult.

WE SAW in a snowy January: skeins of commuting geese, blue tit, wren, buzzard.

MAP OS Explorer **344**, Pentland Hills, Penicuik & West Linton

SHORT CUT: If time is short you can start by walking along the westish tarmac road to the wide crossroads mentioned in Leg 5. This will cut approx. 3km or 45' from the statistics.

Distance 13km	Short cut 10km
Ascent 350m	100m
Walking Time 3h51'	3h 15'
Allow 5h	4h 15'
Highest elevation 370m	

PARK on the roadside by the trees on the Lamancha road at GR NT232 4945 near Shiplaw Farm.

TO GET THERE Follow the A703 S from Leadburn for about 4 miles. Turn R on to the Lamancha road. About 1 mile later you pass Shiplaw Farm. Soon the road bends suddenly R. Park by the trees.

TOILETS informal in the trees!

CAFÉ Whitmuir Organic Place, GR NT192 511, for lunch. If you are a big group it is best to let them know the day before that you are coming. 01968 661 908.

Above the complex is a plant centre. In the main building is an art gallery displaying the work of Scottish artists and crafts people. An organic shop is partially stocked from the farm. In the fields look out for pigs, hens and cattle enjoying the outdoor life.

THE WALK

1   **1.3km; 0m; 19'**
    Take the old Edinburgh to Moffat Post Road S towards Eddleston. After 1.3km, 19', you reach a 4 way junction. Turn R, W.
    GR NT2327 4819.   1.3km; 0m; 19'

2   **0.8km; 30m; 15'**
    Soon pass through a sheep fold and into the rough field beyond. Use the best route you can through the rushes to reach the gate in the NW corner. Go through into the moorland.
    GR NT2252 4845.   2.1km; 30m; 34'

3   **0.4km; 25m; 9'**
    Head for the sparse wooded area to the W. The W side

of this is on top of Cloich Rig. Turn R, just E of N along the Rig to the fence. Cross it where you can.
GR NT2217 4846.   2.5km; 55m; 43'

4   0.9km; 35m; 17'

Go some 350m further along the Rig, passing a prehistoric ring, to find an ill-defined track heading down, L, N of W-ish, towards the Early Burn and a band of trees. Descend and cross the stream and fence as you can. Ascend through the next 2 fields to reach the farm track close to Cloich Farm. Turn R, NE-ish
GR NT217 4905   3.4km; 90m; 1h

5   2km; 30m; 33'

Follow the farm access road for some 900m, 13' to a wide cross roads. Turn L. The short cut joins here. Walk right through the forest, about a km, to reach a multi-junction on the other side.
GR NT213 502.   5.4km; 120m; 1h33'

6   0.5km; 10m; 8'

Take the least defined L, 240°, track at the edge of the trees. Follow this soggy way to a gate into the forest again. Go through the pedestrian gate and immediately turn R, NW by the fence.
GR NT2084 500   5.9.km; 130m; 1h41'

7   1.2km; 80m; 26'

This leg is over rough tussocky ground with overhanging branches. Be careful with your footing. Go over the rise and then follow the fence down to where a fire tower oversees a slippery bridge across a stream. Once across step over the handrail fence so it is on your right. Continue to follow it. Soon you have to leap across another burn in a little gorge. On the other side climb up by the fence to the end of the forest area at a transverse fence. Enjoy the views.
GR NT1995 509   7.1km; 210m; 2h07'

8   1.3km; 5m; 20'

Follow the transverse fence SW-ish slightly up. Pause to enjoy the views.
Now go down to the gate* at GR NT1955 5055. Go through this awkward gate into the fields. Once in the fields follow the curving track NW-ish as it rushes downhill through the gates to Whitmuir Organic Place. Enjoy your refreshment.
GR NT191 512.   8.4km; 215m; 2h27'

To the W you can see the village of West Linton. Going S, L from there comes Mendick Hill with Ingraston Hill leading up to it. Over them you can see the Pentlands drawing to a close in the Dunsyre Hills. To the SW are the lumpy summits of the Dolphinton Hills. Turning to look almost due N you see the flattish top of the highest Pentland peak, Scald Law. Just S of it is South Black Hill. To the N is Carnethy, the second highest.

Off the beaten track

9 1.3km; 110m; 31'
Return up the steep hill to the gate* mentioned in leg 8.
Go through. Continue SE-ish across the rough woodland
area, over boggy bits and streams, to clamber up to a
broad track. Turn L, E.
GR NT199 5021   9.7km; 325m; 2h58'

10 1.2km; 5m; 19'
Follow the track as it goes SE and then E past the ruin
of Grassfield and finally reaches the pedestrian gate you
used on your outward journey.
GR NT208 500   10.9km; 330m; 3h17'

11 2.1km; 20m; 34'
Go straight ahead to the multi junction where you were
at the end of Leg 5. GR NT213 502. Take the SE track
out of it to retrace your steps to the other side of the
forest and the broad crossroads mentioned in Leg 5.
Now leave the outward route to go straight ahead on the
tarmac road. Pass the old observatory on your L which
once belonged to Edinburgh University but has been a
private home since 2006. It changed hands for around
£100,000. Continue to your car.
                                    13km; 350m; 3h51'

Tree Creeper

119

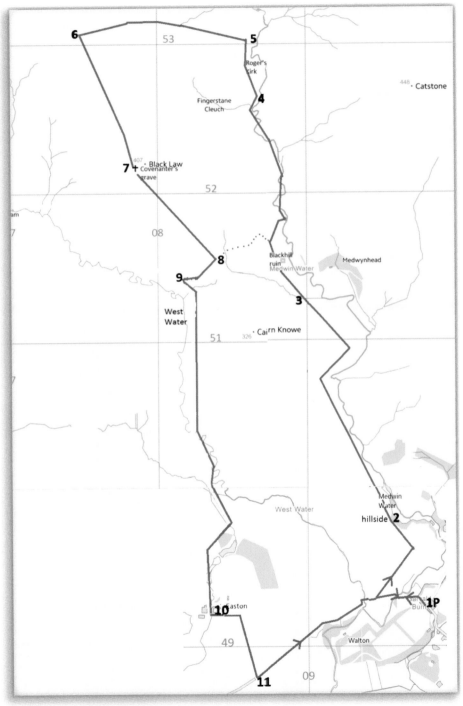

Not to scale

25 • THE LAST STEPS OF THE COVENANTER

An atmospheric walk tracing the last kilometres of John Carphin who was wounded at the Battle of Rullion Green and died out here on the bleak Pentland Hills. For maximum empathy do this walk in November or December.

Goldfinch

WE SAW, in October: Buzzard, 3 snipe, hundreds of commuting geese, large flock of finches, dipper, raven.

MAP OS Explorer **344**, The Pentland Hills, Penicuik, West Linton

Distance 13km
Ascent 300m
Walking Time 4h
Allow 5h
Highest elevation 405m

PARK at Garvald Home Farm. GR NT0985 4925. For permission to park ring 01968 682238.

TO GET THERE Go S on A702, Biggar Road. Just after the sign for Dolphinton take the right turn indicating Dunsyre and Garvald. About 1km later take the R turn indicated Garvald. Follow this road to Garvald Home Farm ignoring turns to Easter and Wester Garvald. Park considerately where there is a space.

TOILETS None

BLACK MOUNT CHURCH at DOLPHINTON EH46 7AD
To get access to the church ring 01968 373180 at least one day ahead.

CAFÉ The Big Red Barn ML12 6QZ. 01968 682291. To get there go 1.5mls further out on the A702 beyond Dolphinton, it is on the L, easily seen. Very welcoming, but if you're a large group, ring the day before.

THE WALK

You are on the west side of the watershed here. The Medwin makes its way to the Irish Sea via the Clyde.

1   **1km; 30m; 18'**
    Leave the farmyard by the pedestrian gate and path at the NW corner of the steading, signposted 'Covenanter's Grave'. Go down and cross the footbridge over the Medwin Water.

Ascend to the E/W path at the top of the field* (you will return through this field). Turn R, E. You will find 2 gates on your L. Use the second one to enter the field on your L, N. Go NW-ish across this field on a faint track, through the gate and across the next field to its N corner. Climb the fence where there is no barbed wire. You are on the hillside.
GR NT095 498   1km; 30m; 18'

2   2.1km; 75m; 40'
The Medwin Water is on your right. Staying on top of the bank, roughly follow it N for almost 2km using any convenient buggy tracks. Near the top, as you come over the crest of a hill, watch for the trees surrounding the now derelict Medwynhead Farm on the other side of the Water. Directly opposite the end of the trees look for the ruin of Blackhill Farm on your side of the stream. There is a solitary stunted rowan tree in the 'garden'. It's job – to keep evil spirits away.
GR NT088 5155   3.1km; 105m; 58'

3   1.3km; 65m; 27'
Continue N to join a broad track. Turn R on to it as it goes N and then curves down to the Medwin Water. Don't cross the stream but instead take the path beside it heading N. A large pipeline carrying water down from the hills accompanies your route. In itself it is not beautiful but it is covered with spectacular lichen. Pause to have a look. Continue up the valley for about 1km when you should find the steep sided Fingerstane Cleuch coming in from the L, W. Just beyond it a fence comes down to your path. It is your marker to leave the path. Stay on the south side of it.
GR NT087 527   4.4km; 170m; 1h25'

4   0.5km; 50m; 13'
Scramble up the bank beside the fence keeping it on your R. As the incline slackens you will find a flatter area, a sort of promontory on your right. This is known as Roger's Kirk, a secret meeting place for the Covenanters in those feuding times. From here they could watch for intruders coming from any direction. Continue to follow the fence for another 300m.
GR NT086 531   4.9km; 220m 1h38'

5   1.1km; 55m; 20'
Pause and look due W. Identify the highest point on the next ridge. You are going to walk N of the boggy area in a W-ish arc around the upper reaches of Fingerstane Cleuch and its associated bogginess to that high point.

Blackhill is the farm where John Carphin asked for help in the night of 28/29 Nov 1666. He was a covenanter from Galloway who was seriously wounded at the Battle of Rullion Green (Walk 15) but managed to escape and started to make his way back to his homeland. During that bitter night he stumbled upon this remote farm. Adam Sutherland, a herd, offered to take him in but in those harsh times that act could have brought disaster to the farm. John Carphin accepted food and water and, knowing that his strength was waning, he asked the shepherd, were he to die, to bury him within sight of his own western hills. He left and limped on up the West Water. In the morning Adam Sutherland found his body at Oaken Dean. He duly carried the corpse up Black Law and when he could see the hills of Ayrshire and Galloway, away to the SW, he buried him.

Buzzard

Further along the E/W track which you are leaving is Oaken Bush where the Covenanter breathed his last on that cold November morning. (Walk 8)

Larch Cones

After about a kilometre of rough going you should be at the highest point with the land beginning to drop away in front.

GR NT076 531　　　　　　　　　　6km; 275m; 1h58'

6　0.9km; 0m; 7'

Turn to head just E of S. Stay on the broad ridge until you see a tall direction pole directly S of you and slightly lower down. Head towards it and watch for a path through the heather. About 100m before the direction pole you should find the Covenanter's Grave marked by a headstone with an inscription which, strangely, does not bear his name.

GR NT078 522　　　　　　　　　　6.9km; 275m; 2h05'

This is not the original stone. The one Adam Sutherland put there was small simply saying "A Covenenter Dunsyre 1666". More of this anon. By the early 18 hundreds the Covenantor's story had become myth-like and was doubted by the son of the farmer who owned the land. The lad took a spade, came up here and dug up the grave. He found the skull, bones and buttons and carried them triumphantly home. His father, a devout Presbyterian, thrashed him and reburied the remains. He vowed to give the grave a proper stone – the one you see today. It was erected in cooperation with Dunsyre Church around 1840.
On a clear day you can see the Galloway/Ayrshire hills away to the SW past the W side of Bleak West Law.

7　0.9km; 0m; 14'

Follow the buggy track and marker poles S to the main E/W track.

GR NT 083 5155　　　　　　　　　7.8km; 275m; 2h19'

8　0.2km; 0m; 14'

Turn R, W for about 200m to the junction with a broad track heading S along the West Water. Turn L on to it.

GR NT 081 515　　　　　　　　　　8km; 275m; 2h33'

9　2.7km; 0m; 40'

Follow the West Water track S for about 2km, 30'. Near a belt of storm-wrecked trees take the R, W fork. Enter the field at the corner of the wood and continue down through the rough pasture to the farmyard of Easton Farm. This was the home of the young grave despoiler of the 19th century.

GR NT 0838 4925　　　　　　　　10.7km; 275m; 3h13'

10　0.6km; 0m; 9'

Walk down through the farmyard and, bear L on to the entrance track. Follow it to where the metalled road begins.

GR NT 087 5488.　　　　　　　　11.3km; 275m; 3h22'

11 1.3km; 20m; 22'

Turn L, E to follow the track, not the road. About 1km
later the track deviates to use a footbridge instead of a
ford. Go across the bridge and through the next gate
or over the stile. The next gate takes you to the field*
crossed in Leg 1. Go down it to the footbridge which
leads you back to your car.

12.6km; 295m; 3h44

But the journey is not over. Drive to Black Mount Church
in Dolphinton. To get there, avoiding awkward R turns,
retrace your way to the T junction. Turn R and follow
signs to Dolphinton. The church is on the L just before
you reach the A702. Here, in the church you can view
the original grave stone. In the graveyard lies the leader
of the Covenanters' cavalry, Major Joseph Learmont, who
survived the Battle of Rullion Green.
(See walk 15)

The original Covenanters' grave stone
with Larry the photographer

124

26 • THREE BRETHERN from YARROWFORD

A visit, approaching from the South, to the 3 great stones which mark the boundaries of 3 great estates. Return along the ridge on the Southern Upland Way for some distance. Then a descent through slopes clad in heather and rowan on the Minchmoor Drove Road.

Peacock on Knapweed

WE SAW in August: buzzard, eyebright, wild pansy, sneezewort, harebells and blooming heather everywhere. If it was in a previously burnt patch the heather had unusual hues. Here and there were plants of the lucky white stuff. Rowan in berry.

MAP OS Explorer **337** and **338**

Distance 13.6km
Ascent 563m
Walking Time 4h30'
Allow 5h30'
Highest elevation 523m

PARK In the lay-by in Yarrowford on the S side of A708 beside an old red telephone box. The PRIVATE sign refers to the garden space not the parking lot. GR NT408 300

TO GET THERE Take the A7 south from Edinburgh. Some 3 miles south of Stow take the R turn indicated Clovenfords. From the roundabout in Clovenfords take A72 exit but immediately turn L on Caddonfoot Road. About a mile later you are joined by the A707. Go ahead by the Tweed for a couple of miles. Cross the Tweed at the light-controlled bridge still on the A707. About 3 miles later, in the outskirts of Selkirk, the road does a sharp L bend. Just after it turn R on to the A708, St Mary's Loch Road. Follow this past the Waterwheel Café and Salmon Viewing Centre on the L, the entrance to Philipshaugh estate on the R, then Bowhill on the L and finally reach Yarrowford.

TOILETS None

CAFÉ The Waterwheel Cafe, 01750 22258, back along the A708 on the R beside the Salmon Viewing Centre.

THE WALK

1   **1.5km; 100m; 33'**
    Walk back along the A708 for about 400m. Just before the bridge turn L, N. 50m later on the right you will

125

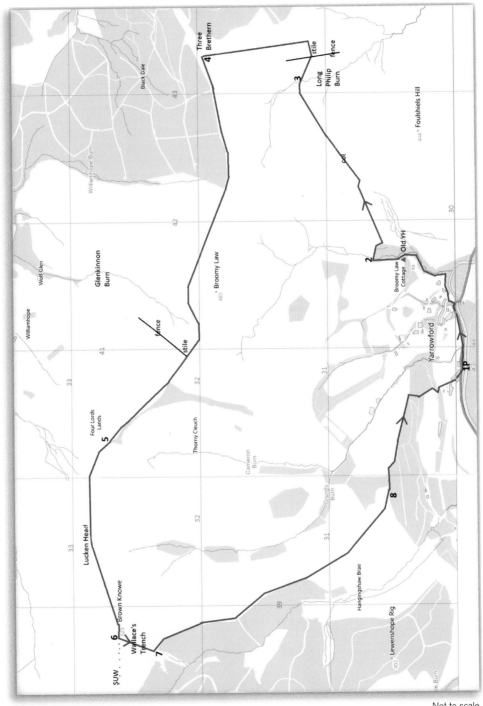

Not to scale

*The Hostel was originally
4 cottages which were
converted to form the first
SYHA hostel. It opened on
2 May 1931. It closed in
Oct 2013 having been sold
for around £200,000. It is a
private dwelling once again.
Before it closed you could
ring ahead and the warden
would make an excellent
cream tea for large groups
but even that was not enough
to turn its fortunes round.*

find the house called the Old Neuk and to the R, S of
its entrance you will find a path running E beside a pig
paddock. Follow the path upwards through woodland
above the gorge of the Old Broadmeadows Burn.
The second and last house on your left is the old
Broadmeadows Youth Hostel. After about 1km you exit
the wood by a big, metal farm gate.
GR NT417 306   1.5km; 100m; 33'

2   1.9km; 160m; 45'
Turn R, E to cross the Old Broadmeadows Burn on a
raised walkway. The path leads you round the end of the
wood and just as it turns S you will find a broad track on
the L ascending Foulshiels Hill. Pause and look S across
the Yarrow to see the ruined top of Newark Tower poking
through the trees.

*Newark is really New Wark as opposed to Auld Wark which was the
original tower. This 'new' tower dates from 1475. In 1645 after the
Marquis of Montrose's army was defeated at the Battle of Philiphaugh
the victorious Covenanters imprisoned and then shot many Royalist
troops in the Tower. (Walk 1)
Opposite Newark Tower on the North side of the A807 is Foulshiels
farmhouse where, in 1771, Mungo Park, the explorer, was born. His
book 'Travels in the Interior of Africa', published in 1799, gave a
realistic account of his experiences as he explored the River Niger.*

Continuing on your journey turn L, E-ish to begin the
hard work of ascending Foulshiels Hill. Pause to rest
and enjoy the views as you go. Once over the crest your
route takes you down and across the Long Philip Burn.
GR NT432 311   3.4km; 260m; 1h18'

*The 3 cairns, each with
its own distinctive shape,
were built in the 16th
century by the lairds of Yair,
Philiphaugh and Selkirk to
mark the meeting point of
their 3 estates.
The horizontal board
honours the standard bearers
of the annual Common
Ridings of the estate
boundaries. The board is by
The Mouseman; you can see
his signature carving at the
end of the board.*

3   1.3km; 120m; 32'
Continue on the path up the far bank to the fence and
over the stile on to Cairn Rig. Follow the soggy path
E-ish for another 200m or so to a cross roads with a much
bigger S/N track. Turn L, N and ascend to the 3 Brethren.
GR NT433 319   4.7km; 380m; 1h50'

4   3.4km; 50m; 56'
You are now on the Southern Upland Way. Turn L, W-ish
and follow this old drove road as it undulates through a
fence, then round the shoulder of Broomy Law and over
another fence. From just beyond the stile, if you look NE-
ish, you can see down the valley of the Glenkinnon Burn
to the village of Yair on the Tweed. Beyond it rise the
Moorfoot Hills. Walk on past the band of trees on your L
to reach the next fence at Four Lords Lands.
GR NT403 327   8.1km; 430m; 2h46

'5   1.6km; 133m; 38'

Beyond the fence ignore the faint track which goes
straight ahead and, instead, follow the SUW slightly
to the R, NW-ish up over Lucken Head to the summit
of Brown Knowe, GR NT3875 3265. 150m ahead
watch for the beginning of Wallace's Trench. Its western
mound is very obvious beside the track. You are going to
descend it.
GR NT387 3265   9.7km; 563m; 3h24'

6   300m; 0m; 15'

Descend with great care. There are many impediments
to contend with: long grass, drains, bracken, heather and
dwarf willow. At the discontinuity, about 100m down,
go a few steps to your R, W to pick up the route of
the Trench again. Having descended 80m altitude in a
distance of 300m you will emerge on to the Minchmoor
Road. The Trench continues, ever steeper, below the
road but luckily you do not have to follow it. You turn L,
SE-ish.
GR NT 386 3235   10km; 563m; 3h39'

7   2.4km; 0m; 36'

After this stressful descent you are rewarded with the
easy, beautiful descent of Hangingshaw Rig following
the Minchmoor Road. You pass through glorious heather
moors dotted with rowan and below you to your L, W
the valley of the Gruntly Burn. Ahead across the Yarrow
valley you can see the cairn on Newark Hill. This marks
the passage of the Duchess' Drive in the Buccleuch
Estate (Walk 1). After 2.4km (36') and a couple of zig
zags you reach Hangingshaw Wood.
GR NT 399 305   12.4km; 563m; 4h15'

8   1.2km; 0m; 18'

Turn L, W-ish alongside the wood on an increasingly big
track. Pass through 2 field boundaries. After about 700m
(10') you reach a further field boundary. Here turn R, S
through a gate into the wood. Descend with the track for
some 250m to reach a crossroads. Go straight ahead,
S, on a narrow path down some steps. At the bottom
turn R and, a few yards further, L on to the metalled road.
Pass some suburban houses on the R and the bright red
village hall on the L to gain the A708. Cross the road to
your car.
                                      13.6km; 563m; 4h33'

*In the distant past several
roads made their way along
this hillside in different eras.
Close to the present SUW
ran an old drove road;
100m down the slope the
Old Minchmoor Road ran
roughly E/W across Scotland.
This point is marked by
a discontinuity in the
earthworks. At this longitude
the roads were crossing from
the Yarrow Ward to the
Ettrick Ward so it is possible
that at this earthwork,
called Wallace's Trench, a
toll was paid or some other
administrative task was
carried out. You can imagine
the cattle bunching up behind
the dyke while the border
formalities were completed.*

*Montrose's Royalist army
limped away up this track
from their defeat at Battle of
Philipshaugh in 1645.*

27 • TORPICHEN, CAIRNPAPPLE, BOWDEN HILL

A walk with several historical sites, a mini ridge, beautiful mixed woodland and long range views. Some soggy bits.

Red Admiral

MAP OS EXPLORER **249** Falkirk, Cumbernauld and Livingston

Distance 13.1km
Ascent 425m
Walking Time 4hrs05'
Allow 5hrs
Highest elevation 240m

PARK in Community Education Car Park in Torphichen near the Perceptory. Grid Ref 968726.

TO GET THERE Take M9 to Junction 3. Go left on A803 to Linlithgow. Drive through the town past the palace. At the next roundabout go L on the A706 indicating Lanark. At next roundabout take second exit still on A706 towards Lanark. About 2.5miles later go left on to minor road B792 indicating Torphichen. (If you reach the A801 you've gone a bit too far. Retrace your route a short distance and watch for the minor B792 on your right.) As you reach Torphichen turn L on Greenside just before the park. At the end of the park turn R on to Bowyett. Again at the end of the park find the Community Centre parking area.

TOILETS At the back of the car park is the Community Education Building. At the left end of the building behind a red door there are toilets. Sometimes they are open.

THE WALK

The Perceptory was the Scottish headquarters of the Knights of St John, aka Knights Templar, founded in 1113 to support the Crusaders. Their leader was a prior; his second in command a preceptor: hence the name perceptory. King David founded this preceptory of which only fragments remain. St John's Ambulance Brigade was set up by the Knights Templar in Victorian times

1 **0.7km; 25m; 0h13'**
Walk past the Perceptory to T junction with Victoria Jubilee Monument. Go L uphill to crossroads. Turn L, E along Cathlaw Lane towards Cairnpapple.
GR NS971 7219   0.7km; 25m; 0h13'

2 **1.3km; 70m; 0h27'**
Pass suburban houses on L and the road begins to ascend with a wooded area on the right. You have to go up into that wooded area. To find the best place watch for a field gate on your left. Immediately opposite, to the left of a beech bush and under a large ash tree, you will find a badger track. Climb up and follow their tracks

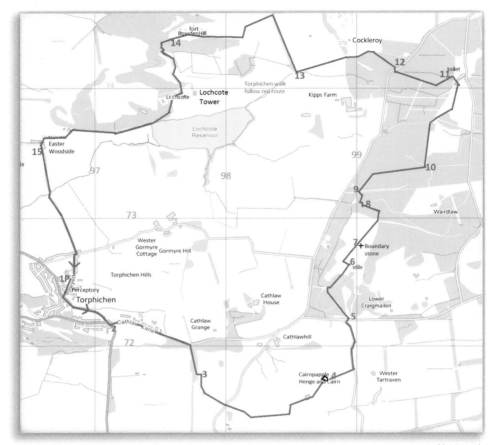

Not to scale

Corral

through the trees to a find a barbed wire fence. Squeeze
through or climb over. The badger track continues up
through the woodland on the raised bank. Follow it.
Wherever the path forks take the left hand, upper option.
Just beyond a mini gorge the left hand path is faint but
follow it all the same up along the bank of the gorge.
Go on until your way is blocked by vegetation. Cross the
fence on your left.
GR NS9775 717   2km; 95m; 0h40'

3   1.1km; 60m; 0h23'
Continue upwards along the margin of the field to the
gate. Climb over, cross road, cross cattle grid and follow
track to mast. Pass it and enter field through a gate. Turn
L along fence. Cross pasture to Cairnpapple gate. Enter
site and explore. The information boards explain the site
and its history. Exit at SE corner by kissing gate.
GR NS9878 7175   3.1km; 155m; 1h03'

4   0.6km; 0m; 0h9'
Cross field on 67° along a faint path to steps. Descend
to road. Turn L, walk up round corner and descend to find
branch road down to right. Go down and cross road at
bottom to kissing gate.
GR NS989 7221   3.7km; 155m; 1h12'

5   0.5km; 25m; 0h10'
Go through gate and follow path through new trees
veering left, up and down to T junction and fence ahead.
Turn R. Ascend NE-ish through new trees to stile. Cross
and go ahead, NNW-ish, on narrow path under trees.
GR NS9905 7261   4.2km; 180m; 1h22'

6   0.4km; 30m; 0h09'
A few metres further as you leave trees turn R, NE, to
ascend ridge of Witch's Hill to a corral built with local
stones. Opposite to the E, across the little valley, beside the
wall is a Perceptory boundary stone with a double cross
cut into it.
GR NS990 7271   4.6km; 210m; 1h31'

Boundary stone with
Cross of Lorraine

7   0.5km; 0m; 0h08'
Continue along and down ridge. {To cut out part of the
very steep descent at the end of the ridge you can use
the lower path between the ridge and the wall.} Continue
down with fence on right to bottom of hill. Ignore stile
part way down. At bottom turn left following fence to
crossroads of paths. Turn R to complicated stile.
GR NS9901 7311   5.1km; 210m; 1h39'

8 0.2km; 5m; 0.04'

Cross and follow path left. After a few metres it goes
sharp right and ascends to junction with track.
GR NS9905 732   5.3km; 215m; 1h43'

9 0.6km; 30m; 0h12'

Go through large gate on R. You are entering Beecraigs
Country Park. Follow broad track ahead to T junction and
sign to Balvormie. Turn L, N.
GR NS995 7338   5.9km; 245m; 1h55'

10 0.6km; 0m; 0h12'

300m, 4' later reach a wide T junction on edge of
meadow. Cross on to path across meadow to fence. Turn
left on path for a few metres. Where it leaves the fence
you go R off the path. Walk over the brow of the little hill
and down to barbecue circles. Pass between barbecue
circles and go ahead into woods to toilet block. Your next
path is on the left as you approach the toilet block.
GR NS997 741   6.5km; 245m; 2h07'

Deadly Nightshade

11 0.6km; 0m; 0h09'

Follow path WSW marked by blue walker signs leading
you through the wind-devastated woods. After about 5
minutes or so come to a crossroads of paths. Turn R. You
are on a little ridge. Ahead take whichever paths keep
you on this little ridge until you reach the road at
GR NS993 741. (The road curves sharply left just below
you on the left). Cross road and up the bank opposite.
GR NS9925 7415   7.1km; 245m; 2h16'

12 1km; 20m; 17'

You need to cross this wooded area in a NWerly
direction. Take whichever paths will achieve this. The
path may have lots of fallen trees like hurdles across it.
Don't let that put you off. On the N side leave the forest
by a gate. Do not take the path ahead up Cockleroy but
turn left, SW-ish. Descend for 150m and pass through a
gate. Continue to descend across the field in a SW-ish
direction to the SW corner of the field where you will find
a signpost. Take the track to the R indicating Linlithgow.
GR NS98505 741   8.1km; 265m; 2h33'

13 1.4km; 90m; 30'

Ascend on this track almost due N for about 500m. At
the crest of the hill you reach a crossroads of paths. Turn
L in a W-ish direction.
Follow this path up over a small hill and down again.

This is Bowden Hill Fort dating from the Bronze Age. It is contemporary with the fort on Cockleroy which lies behind you to the East (Walk 20). The Bowden fort is the bigger of the two and is reputed to be where King Arthur defeated the Saxons in the 6th century. In the woods on the north side of the fort are the old limekilns from which the railway track led to the canal at Linlithgow.

Lochcote Castle was a 17th century building which occupied the whole of this green area. The stub of building remaining is from an angle tower of the original castle with a more recent addition on top to make it a doocot. At some point the castle burned down and was replaced by an enormous Lochcote House on the same site. Around 1850 there are records of plans by a Mrs Derby to take down parts of the house and by the end of the 19th century it had been completely replaced by a stable block. There is a remnant of this at the N side of the site. Half buried in the grass there are many large blocks of stone from the demolition. There is no evidence of when the present house was built but it seems likely that Mrs Derby built herself the present more manageable house on the elevated site with a view. Where you are standing, she had her huge stable block for horses and carriages.

You are walking on the track of an old railway which used to carry lime from kilns in the north face of Bowden Hill to the canal at Linlithgow. It was abandoned early in the 20th century.

At about the lowest point find a gate on your left going into a boggy area. Go through and across the boggy area towards the bank of trees. Find an indistinct path ascending steeply in a westward direction. Climb up passing outlying stones of the Bowden Hill fort which you reach at the top of the ascent.
GR NS977 744   9.5km; 355m; 3h03'

14 2.3km; 25m; 0h37'
Find an exit from the fort area to the west, possibly through a fence, and descend steeply to join a broader track which curves down from SW to S to enter a field through a gate. Look for an indistinct path heading SE-ish at first as it contours round a little hill. Reach a gate on the S side of the field. Go through into woodland. A few steps further, beyond some rhododendrons, you reach a fairly open area. On your R you can see a large house. You are standing where its predecessor, Lochcote Castle, and its stables stood.
Head west to come out of the woods on a track at the gate of the large house. Enter its grounds and leave by following its access road to a tarmac road.
GR NS9656 7356   11.8km; 380m; 3h40'

15 1.3km; 45m; 0h25'
Go ahead S on tarmac road, down and up to Torphichen. Cross road and find car park ahead.
                                13.1km; 425m; 4h05'

133

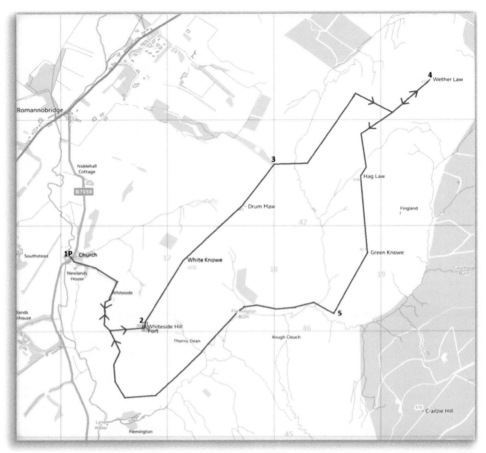

Not to scale

28 • WETHER LAW

A hill walk with a high mountain feel accessed through a large prehistoric site.

WE SAW in August: whin chat, curlew, small heath butterfly.

MAP OS Explorer **336**, Biggar & Broughton, Culter Fell & Dollar Law

Distance 12.5km
Ascent 648m
Walking Time 4h12'
Allow 5h15'
Highest elevation 479m

The present Newlands Church was built in 1838. The ruin 100m further south along the road has been the site of a church since Saxon times, 5-6th century. In the parish records there are minutes dating from 1650.

PARK In the car park opposite Newlands Church, Romannobridge GR NT161 467

TOILETS None.

TO GET THERE Take the A701 south, either via Auchendinny or Penicuik, to Romannobridge. Turn L on to B7059. About 1ml later find Newlands Church car park on the right.

CAFÉ Whitmuir Farm 01968 661147. GR NT191 511. To get there return N on A701. Just beyond the speed bumps to warn of a bend in the road watch for the entrance to Whitmuir and the Dancing Light Gallery on the right.

Marsh Orchid

Snowy descent

THE WALK

1   1.4km; 178m; 39'

Cross the road and just south of the church take the track uphill through the trees signposted, first Newlands House and then Peebles. Ignoring any turns to the left, emerge into the open and swing southish to pass Whiteside Cottage. Beyond the cottage to the SW you pass through a gate. Pause to look up at the skyline to the SE-ish. The bumpy profile indicates the presence of Whiteside Hill Fort, your destination for this leg. To get there follow the wall on your left as it zigzags S and then SE. Join the lower wall and zig zag with it S and then SE and E up the hill by the track obvious a few metres from the corner. Leave it at the top corner where it turns N. Continue to ascend E-ish and enter the fort by its SW gate.

GR NT168 461   1.4km; 178m; 39'

2   2km; 120m; 42'

Leave the fort by the NE exit and cross the earthwork on the path which leads up over White Knowe and on across Drum Maw. Enjoy the 360° views. Descend Drum Maw keeping beside a wall running NE-ish. Ignore any turnings. At the south tip of a strip of forest you cross a track. Stop at the lower edge of the trees.

GR NT180 476 (this is the vantage point* referred to in Leg 3). Pause here to look across the Fingland Burn to the hillside beyond where you will see a track across the hillside running S to N. Towards the NE you will see it disappear round the shoulder of the hill. In the next leg you will leave the path at this point. The mast on the skyline is not your destination. The trig point on Wether Law is N of the mast, which is actually on Hag Law. The trig point is on a bearing of about 60° from your present position.

GR NT180 476   3.4km; 298m; 1h21'

3   1.9km; 190m; 48'

Descend steeply still beside the wall, through a fence, across the burn and up the hill to gain the S/N track mentioned above. Turn L, N-ish, and follow it as it goes up the valley side for less than 1km (12'). Stop as it rounds the shoulder mentioned in Leg 2. Opposite you can see the wall marking the southern boundary of a forest which has been logged. Look back to the strip of forest you paused beside in the previous leg. Your vantage point* at its lowest corner should be out of sight. All these clues establish where you leave the track.

Whiteside Hill Fort had its natural defensive position reinforced in prehistoric times, at first by one rampart which protected nine 'houses', and later by another double rampart. It then fell into disrepair, probably at the time of the Roman occupation. After the Latins had left, the local people returned and built another, this time stone, structure within the area enclosed by rampart one. The earthwork connecting the fort to the slopes of White Knowe is contemporary with rampart 1.

Frog

Ascend R, E, steeply up to the ridge GR NT1881 4830. As you zig zag up, avoiding the bracken, stay roughly in line with the forest boundary wall behind you on the opposite side of the valley. On the ridge turn L, NE-ish, to reach the trig point of Wether Law.
GR NT195 484   5.3km; 488m; 2h09'

4   2.7km; 50m; 45'
Follow the ridge path all the way back S-ish over Hag Law, with its mast, over Green Knowe and finally down to the Flemington Burn.
GR NT186 462   8km; 538m; 2h54'

5   4.5km; 110m; 1h18'
Turn R, W-ish, with the track following the burn downstream. You are now on a Tweed Walkway track with marker posts. Follow these for the rest of your journey, round the bases of Drum Maw and White Knowe, around the shoulder of Whiteside Hill, past Whiteside Cottage and down to your car.
12.5km; 648m 4h12'

Notes

1. Bowhill ....
   ....

2. Cardrona ....
   ....

3. Circuit of St Mary's Loch ....
   ....

4. Cockburn Law, Edin's Hall Broch ....
   ....

5. Corehouse and Falls of Clyde ....
   ....

6. Craig an Uamhaidh, Craigvinean..
   ....

7. Culter Fell...
   ....

8. Dunsyre Hills...
   ....

9. Eddleston Circular..
   ....

10. Eddleston to Peebles via Glentress ....
    ....

11. End of the Antonine Wall ....
    ....

12. Glengabber ....
    ....

13. Glenlude and the Southern Upland Way ....
    ....

14. Harehead Hill and Tibbie Tamson's Grave..
    ....

Notes

15. History in the Pentlands ....
....

16. Lammer Law and Hopes Reservoir ....
....

17. Learmont Drysdale Memorial ....
....

18. Loch Ordie and Deuchary Hill..
....

19. Mendick Hill..
....

20. Muiravonside and Beyond ....
....

21. Nine Mile Burn to Carlops - two ways...
....

22. Portmore Snowdrops...
....

23. Rough Castle and the Falkirk Wheel..
....

24. Shiplaw to Whitmuir Return ....
....

25. The Last Steps of the Covenanter..
....

26. Three Brethern from Yarrowford...
....

27. Torpichen ....
....

28. Wether Law..
....

Printed in Poland
by Amazon Fulfillment
Poland Sp. z o.o., Wrocław